Who Cheats More
Than A Politician?™

Who Cheats More Than A Politician?™

Venoria Todman

Mystique Journal

Miami, Florida

ISBN-13: 978-0-692-36078-1

Edited by Venoria Todman

Co-Edited by Susan Cambridge, et.al

Published by Mystique Journal

Printed in the United States of America

Acknowledgement

Inspired by real Couples who were hurting and needed their stories told, in hope that someone will benefit and will not be a victim or remain in an insufferable situation. Sharing their stories provided them with a voice and freedom to express their inner thoughts and feelings. They are happy to know that someone cared enough to listen and I am happy to impart their stories to the masses, in hope that the readers will be inspired and men and women across the world would be empowered to let their voices be heard.

Firstly, I give thanks to God for the gift of writing and for seeing me through those late nights when I was compiling this book's contents, and at times felt alone. He never left my side. **Special thanks** to those of you who encouraged me while writing this book and those who gave insight, no matter how insignificant it may have seemed at the time. Most importantly, **I am thankful for my beautiful and loving family** (Gerald, Alvan, Trisha, & Dion), in supporting and uplifting me, when I felt like giving up. Your strength and undeniable love encouraged me to pursue this feat and for this, I will be forever grateful.

Preface

For many years I thought about the idea of writing a book but it was not until early 2014 that I decided which topic I wanted to address.

I first thought of the title and then I began writing in April, 2014. Ironically, I was feeling a little down, so I began to express my feelings on paper. I wrote about forty pages in one hour then I stopped.

It was always in my mind to resume writing, but I did not, until a few months following when it was announced in church that one of the members had written a book on marriage and was having a book signing.

I said to myself, "I really need to finish this book," so again, when I returned home I resumed writing. I must admit, at the time I was not very focused but managed to successfully complete twenty five additional pages. This occurred in July, 2014.

The next time I resumed writing was in August, 2014. I was upset with my spouse at the time and we were not conversing, so I reached for the notepad and wrote and wrote. I guess my spouse is a good motivator to get me writing.

I think I lose myself in writing especially when I am upset and that enables me to remain calm. Writing is therapeutic and it has always been that way for me. As I begin to write, the thoughts flow easily and I know exactly how I would like the body of my work to be written.

October, 2014 came and my manuscript was almost completed. Again I thought about the title that I always had in the "back" of my mind. I wanted it to be something that is easy to remember and at the same time, I wanted it to be bold.

I am a firm believer that "greatness is wrapped up in simplicity". Therefore, please do not look for highly sophisticated language or "off the wall" phrases that no one understands.

My objective is for the contents to be the same as the title, to be simple and understandable so that the readers would be able to comprehend it fully and not struggle with complex terminology.

Just to be clear, I do have an Executive MBA degree from the University of Miami, and I have worked as an Adjunct Professor of Value Communication and Business Ethics at Trinity International University. In addition, I do speak to large audiences and senior management of major corporations, as part of my career.

Furthermore, I continue to write every day, so have no fear, I do have a few immense words that I can throw in every now and again for those who may find it appealing, but no, not for this book. This is special to the masses that are comprised of people from all walks of life; it is to you I write.

I thought of whom I wanted my audience to be. Those of you who may be going through tough times, it is to you I write. Those of you who need uplifting, it is to you I write.

I write for each and every person who has had to endure pain and suffering in their relationships and in their families. For those that have had to listen to lies, be lied to and lied on, it is to you I write.

For those that cannot tell if they are being cheated on, to you I write. I thought of each and everyone of you, who is afraid to let your voices be heard and for those of you who are afraid to face reality. For those of you who are afraid to walk away, to you I write.

Let us not forget those who have been falsely accused of cheating and for those who have cheated but are sorry. I write for each of you. Therefore, each of you need to be able to understand what I have written, so you can identify and learn and grow from all the experiences shared. To all of you I write with simplicity and with fun, but at the same time with inspiration.

Now that I have just about completed this book, everywhere I go there is a discussion or a new book on relationships. It appears that this is one of the hottest topics circulating our globe today and is therefore the reason it is being addressed from so many different perspectives.

Everyone seems to be writing and eager to provide their point of view on this relationship wave. I thought to myself, "ok, how many books are going to be launched about the same topic, before I launch mine?"

I am confident though, that despite the fact that there are many books surrounding all types of relationships and marriages, you, the readers, will find this book to be intriguing and unique in its contents, as it was written just for you.

If any of your spouses have ever cheated, just about every situation in this book is relatable. You will be able to assimilate to an extent of what you may have experienced or are experiencing. I encourage you to take your time and read each chapter, page and paragraph.

You will indeed go through the emotions of these couples and feel like you know each and everyone of them. You will empathize and become them for that moment.

Yes, this reading is very powerful, fascinating, captivating and appealing. It is indeed a revelation of who cheats more than a politician.

Foreword

Politicians, for the most part are targeted and ousted by each other and by the public for their illicit indiscretions/affairs. They, of course are not the only ones "doing it" but the spotlight is on them and they have to deal with the backlash.

Having been married for more than three decades and listening to many stories, seeing the pain in the eyes of families, friends and acquaintances, hearing the sadness in the voices, from so many couples, I felt compelled to write this book.

This is a book that chronicles seven married couples, six of which have experienced infidelity. Four of the couples have survived the many challenges they encountered. One couple is divorced with no regrets. Another is contemplating a divorce, or at least a separation.

The seventh couple has a perfect or almost perfect marriage. Therefore, for those of you who are considering marriage, there is hope that you can have full commitment from each other and your marriage can actually work.

My hope for you, the readers, is that these life experiences will help at least one couple to avoid divorce and enable others to be aware of their surroundings and appreciate each other.

I am sure there are many married couples that can identify with each and every one of these situations. I am not claiming to be a marriage counselor, but after each couple's story I will share my perspective/advice on the situation, speaking directly to them, in the event they are reading this book.

You will also read about the emotional affair that continued for approximately two decades with a fantasy couple but they have not crossed the line to physical activity, as most of the years they have been married to different individuals, or have been involved with someone else.

In addition, you will read about my personal story/marriage and how, as a couple, we are still standing, despite the good, bad and the ugly.

For the protection and privacy of the families, their actual names and other personal information will not be disclosed or will have limited disclosure.

Who cheats more than a Politician? Let's keep reading. Enjoy!

TABLE OF CONTENTS

CHAPTER I

<u>INTRODUCTION</u>

As previously stated, politicians, for the most part, are known for cheating. Their infidelities are usually exposed on the national level, as they are public figures. Expectations are generally set high since they are often sought for guidance and exemplary leadership.

We are forgetting, however, that they are human beings and becoming a politician does not change who that person is, or the lifestyle that person lives. The only thing that is different is that they are now viewed by the nation.

I must state that I am not a politician, neither am I related to one. Furthermore I am not condoning or defending their lifestyles. I am simply making an observation and requesting you to do the same. Let us be truthful, we often point the finger to those we do not know and those that are in our lives, we ignore.

CHAPTER II

Internal/External Questions

An important question to ask is, "am I looking into my own life as I scrutinize the details of others' lives?" Have you asked yourself the following questions?

The What Is's

What is my spouse doing?

What is my brother/sister doing?

What is my father/mother doing?

What is my nephew/niece doing?

What is my uncle/aunt doing?

What is my preacher/first lady doing?

What is my deacon/deaconess doing?

What is my best friend doing?

What is my neighbor doing?

The main question is what are you doing?

The Do You's

Do you get a pass because you are an ordinary person and no one knows you?

Do you get a pass because you are not a Christian?

Do you get a pass because you feel no one knows? (Someone always does).

Do you get a pass because the other person is having problems, so you feel it is ok to explore?

Do you get a pass because you do not feel loved by your partner?

Do you get a pass because both of you want it?

Do you get a pass because your partner did it?

Do you get a pass because you wanted to experiment, but it did not mean anything to you?

Do you get a pass because you feel like everyone else is doing it?

Do you get a pass because your best friend did it and did not get caught?

You feel like you are getting away with murder as you think no one knows. Let's say that is true. Have you considered the following?

The What If's

What if my children find out?

What if my spouse finds out?

What if my Christian brothers and sisters find out?

What if my pastor finds out?

What if my parents find out?

What if my boss finds out?

What if my relatives find out?

What if my friends find out?

What if no one finds out?

What if everyone finds out?

Now, let us move on to the "Am I's"

The Am I's

Am I ready to give up on my marriage?

Am I ready to be separated from my children and the life that I have built for them?

Am I ready to be taken to the "cleaners" financially speaking?

Am I ready to endure the shame and guilt?

Am I ready to give up on the affair?

Am I ready for the looks?

Am I ready to face the music?

Am I ready for the judgment?

Am I ready to confess?

Am I ready to seek forgiveness?

We are also faced with the "Randoms".

The "Randoms"

Is the sex worth all the things that I have accomplished, to see it all plummeting down?

The person I am cheating with, is that person also sleeping with others? Who is that person with, when I am not there?

If I leave my spouse and my children for this person, how do I know, this person will not leave me for another person?

Will I get tired of this person that knows I am married and still wants to be with me? Will this person get tired of me?

What type of person is this person really is, considering there is no concern even though I am married?

How did I get myself into this and how can I get out?

Will the person let me go, if I admit that I made a terrible mistake and I do not want this?

Will my spouse be willing to forgive me?

How will I get my spouse to trust me, even if I am forgiven?

Will our marriage ever be the same?

Will I ever be able to look my spouse in the eyes?

Will I be able to say I love you and will I be telling the truth?

After all of the questions you have asked yourself, is it really worth it, to enter into an illicit affair?

Let us look into the tell-tale signs that will help us identify if our partners are engaging in any type of sexual affairs/activities outside of marriage.

CHAPTER III

CHEATING RADAR ALERT QUESTIONS

When someone is cheating, there are always tell-tale signs and you do not have to look too far to find them. In this chapter, I will provide you with some guidance to help you figure it out.

The following outlines a series of questions that you can ask yourself and you will know if your spouse is involved in any type of extra-curricular sexual activities.

Have you experienced the unknown phone calls in the middle of the night and early mornings?

How about the silent text messages or should I say "sext" messages?

Have you been told I have to work late tonight, or I have a special job to do on weekends?

Have you been yelled at, given the silent treatment, or given unfriendly looks for no reason?

Does the cell phone ring continuously when you are out together, and the other person seems afraid to answer and does not look you in the eye?

Have you been told I have to leave "real" early in the morning to meet a customer, or to get an early start in the day?

Have you been avoided in the bedroom and for weeks you do not engage in sexual activity?

How about when you do engage in sexual activity, there is no passion from the other end, and there is more softness than hardness and takes a long time to come full circle?

How about a sensual kiss or any type of kiss? When was the last time you were passionately kissed?

How about being told, if I kiss you on the lips, I am not kissing you anywhere else and if I kiss you anywhere else, I am not kissing you on the lips?

When was the last time you were told you are beautiful or I love you, even when you asked for it to be said?

Have you found unscrupulous things on the cell phone and when confronted, you are told "it is not what you think" and "I am going to get rid of the phone," but never did and continue to lie about it?

How about seeing body parts and the person they belong to, picture, on the phone but is being told "I did not take those pictures."

What about having the phone hidden and continuously on silence?

How about being told out of the blue, "I do not love you anymore, so I am going to move out for a while, but please know it is not because of another woman?"

How about coming home one day, and the person is gone and does not show up for approximately two weeks? When he/she shows up, there is no explanation other than "I was not with anyone."

Have you ever called your spouse's cell phone and the opposite sex answers? Have you ever answered your spouse's cell phone and there is only breathing?

How about your spouse taking a change of clothes to work and returns home smelling like soap or cheap fragrance?

Does your spouse's breath exude an unflattering scent?

How about your spouse comes home and immediately rushes to the shower?

How about your spouse deliberately leaving the cell phone at home and deciding to supposedly work late at night?

Are clothes missing from your spouse's closet, or does your spouse wear clothes that neither of you bought?

How about being away and coming home to find your family picture from your center piece relocated on the refrigerator?

How about finding unknown underwear between your brand new waterbed?

How about finding condoms hidden away and you do not use condoms?

What about finding your spouse's underwear under the driver's seat, and the response is "it felt funny on me so I took it off"?

What about finding the opposite sex jacket in the back of your car and your spouse says, "I am not sure who that belongs to as I did not have anyone in the car"?

How about finding lots of jewelry, makeup, and an electric toothbrush that are not yours, in the front of your car, after returning from a trip?

Let us not forget this one, the "mother" of all, finding a baby bottle in your car, when you do not have a baby!

How about your spouse closing the bathroom door when he hears you approaching?

How about secretly putting rubbing alcohol continuously on body parts when you think no one is looking? What are you treating?

How about looking at the cell phone nonstop and claiming to be looking on the internet for business opportunities?

Considering the radar alert questions, I think you have the picture, but if not, let me spell it out for you. If by chance you are experiencing or have experienced any of the above scenarios, there is a 99.9% probability that your spouse is cheating or has cheated on you. "Who cheats more than a Politician?"

We will now examine the lives of the couples and experience the good, bad, and the estranged.

CHAPTER IV

MR. & MRS. FENCE

Told to me by Mr. Fence's Sister who lives on their property - Americans

Mr. & Mrs. Fence have been married for more than two decades and have five children; (three boys and two girls, ranging from the ages of eight to twenty one). Mr. & Mrs. Fence are both self-employed and Mrs. Fence occasionally does volunteer work at a nearby hospital.

This family has a beautiful home, (with five separate apartment duplexes) that others may desire. They appear to be very successful and are well known in the community. Mrs. Fence is very sweet and reserved and Mr. Fence is very outgoing and overtly friendly.

It happened that an aunt became ill and instead of being sent to hospice, she requested that she be sent home to enjoy the remaining time she has in the privacy of her home. Her home however, is in a very isolated area. Therefore, the Fence's family decided to move her to one of their apartment buildings, so someone could keep a close eye on her. As she is gravely ill, nurses and/or caregivers need to be on-site.

Most of the nurses/caregivers that they employ are usually young and impressionable; some with families and some single. It has been known that Mr. Fence frequently visits and demands entrance to the apartment, while the caregivers are working.

This, of course, is unknown to Mrs. Fence. However, based on her personality, I am not sure if it would make a difference if this information is revealed to her. Something tells me Mrs. Fence would view this as Mr. Fence being concerned and wanting to make sure all is ok with his aunt.

One specific caregiver is known to be his #1 mistress. They have been seen traveling together on several occasions. The sad thing though, is this main mistress has endeared herself into Mrs. Fence's heart and she can do no wrong in her eyes. Mrs. Fence sees her as part of the family but little does she know she is indeed part of the family.

There were times, when the #1 mistress was in the hospital and Mr. Fence was always by her side making sure she received excellent care. Mrs. Fence has a big heart and does not question Mr. Fence, as she trusts him implicitly. One would ask why is Mr. Fence so interested to the point of making it his business to continuously visit the #1 mistress without his spouse.

It has been said that there are three other caregivers that Mr. Fence has been frequently "sexting" and demanding sexual favors. Although two of them have tried to warn Mrs. Fence, she does not believe her spouse will betray her in that way (talk about being "naïve"). Mrs. Fence feels that the "haters" are jealous and are fabricating stories. When is she going to wake up from her sleep?

Mr. Fence apparently buys sex toys and other sexual gadgets for those he desires and when he cannot or does not get his way, he demands that they are replaced. As Mr. Fence believes he is a powerful force, he continues to cheat and intimidates the women that are seemingly weak. He also intimidates his spouse and tells her what she wants to hear. Sadly, she actually believes every word that exudes from his mouth.

Some of the caregivers that have engaged in, or are engaging in sexual activity with Mr. Fence, dress inappropriately, while on the job. One in particular takes it to the extreme, where she wears revealing outfits and is "braless" at times.

Why would a caregiver dress so provocative and why would she be allowed to continue to do so while on the job? Is everyone afraid of Mr. Fence? Is he that powerful of a man?

The main mistress has become very jealous of Mr. Fence's advances towards the other women. She wants to remain #1 and will do anything to secure that position. It is however known, that said mistress has a male domestic partner but still continues to indulge in this illicit affair with Mr. Fence.

Mistress, if you had a daughter, would you like your daughter to be sleeping with a married man? Would you like her spouse to be sleeping with another woman? Stop sleeping with Mr. Fence.

You have a partner, is he not enough for you? You and those who are like you are an embarrassment to women.

It is good to know however, that decent people still exists and not all of the caregivers will "lie down" or succumb to Mr. Fence's advances. Things got out of control as one caregiver was tired of saying "no" to no avail. Mr. Fence knew this person had a fiancé, but still pursued her right under Mrs. Fence's nose.

Feeling sexually harassed, at one point, she became so irate, the caregiver threatened to shoot Mr. Fence, if he did not refrain his sexual advances. Within a month, this caregiver was fired. This should not be. How could he continue to do this and do it so openly?

Those who are aware of what is going on, were appalled of the situation and what he did to this caregiver, who was indeed one of the best they have had. I am at a loss for words, as all of this information was being communicated to me.

The question is continuously being asked how can Mrs. Fence not know what is happening? Where is she when all this is going on? It seems that Mr. Fence is completely in charge of the hiring/firing for the caregivers and he takes advantage of the situation.

This is like a "Lifetime Movie". Why is he not being reported for sexually charged overtures in the workplace? All those he has offended, need to get together and publicize how he is harassing the workers and taking advantage of the less fortunate in his employ. No one should have to endure this.

Let us examine what Mr. Fence has been up to lately. My reliable source tells me he has now spread his wings outside of his property. He is now known as the "sex man" with special powers. Are you kidding me? Women are actually falling for this guy?

My understanding is he is not even "eye candy", so I would venture to say, it must be in his pocket book. I wonder if that is the reason Mrs. Fence is being oblivious to her surroundings. We may never know.

As previously mentioned, Mr. Fence is now known to broaden his horizon and instead of only being with the caregivers on his properties, he is going through the community taking whoever will have him. There seems to be no limit to his madness.

It is said that he now has an additional steady mistress housed on a private property and he consistently visits her unknown to Mrs. Fence. Why is it that the spouse is always the last to know?

Someone needs to bring Mrs. Fence "up to speed". Did she lose her eyesight once she saw his pocket book? How can she not know that the property exists? Eyewitnesses have said that he is often seen coming from the vicinity at night time, while Mrs. Fence is at home, clueless, or pretending to be.

Mr. Fence's affairs and indiscretions are now public knowledge and you would think that Mrs. Fence would listen to the little voice inside her, that something is wrong. We may never understand what goes through so many spouses minds when faced with the obvious.

However, every woman knows when her spouse is cheating, but at times prefers to live in denial, hoping it would fade away. Sadly, it only gets worse.

Ignoring a situation does not make it go away. It empowers the wrong doer to continue doing what he/she has set-out to do.

Mr. Fence has taken it one step further. He has invited some of the mistresses at family gatherings, introducing them as employees to Mrs. Fence and other family members. This apparently happened at an end-of-year event at his home.

Many new faces were there for the first time and Mrs. Fence was no wiser. If I ever become so dense, someone please bring me out of the delusional world. Anyone coming to my house will have to be approved by me. If I do not know you, why must you be at my home?

It is said that just about every time Mr. Fence travels, there is always someone on his arm and most of the time, it is not Mrs. Fence. Does Mrs. Fence not ask where he is going and why? Or is he that good of a con-man that he has plausible answers? Is he that smart of a person that he completely pulls the wool over Mrs. Fence's eyes? Again, why is the spouse always the last to know?

Can someone please tell me if this is a sexual bucket list for Mr. Fence? Perhaps after decades of marriage and five children, Mrs. Fence is no longer interested in sexual activities and would prefer Mr. Fence be serviced by others as she cannot fathom the thought of him climbing on top of her. It does happen.

Moving on, no offense to you, men, who are reading this book, but most men are not thorough and cannot hide things efficiently and effectively. In addition, when they hide things they do not remember where they hid them.

This is where women shine, as most of us are exceptionally smart and can smell a "rat" or hide a "rat". If we do not want our spouses to know something they will not know. We hide things from them all the time, like when we go shopping. Ladies, you know I am telling the truth.

Mrs. Fence, maybe the above theory is actually what is happening with you, but if it is not, please be brave and do not be afraid to confront Mr. Fence. Pay attention, please.

If you sincerely do not know what is going on, please be sure to read the advice page to you at the end of this chapter and you will know. Once you become aware, do not enable him in this behavior and please do not be mad with the "Author" for bringing it to your attention.

My Advice to Mr. & Mrs. Fence

Mrs. Fence, In addition to what I previously said this is my advice to you if you are reading this book. Please stop living in denial and being afraid of what others would say. If you have your own car, which I am sure you do, follow Mr. Fence just for one day or one night and see where he goes.

If you do not desire to do that, because you are afraid of what you will find out and may be tempted to break his leg or run him over, please hire a P.I. (Private Investigator) and secure the proof. It is not that difficult if you put your mind to it. As a matter of fact, you do not have to put much thought into it.

Men are so reckless, they act without thinking and leave clues throughout the house, on their cell-phones, in their cars, just about every where, so be very attentive.

You actually may not need to get in your car to follow him, just visit his sick aunt staying on your property and you would probably find him in a compromising position. Have you ever asked yourself, why is he visiting his aunt so often and staying long hours?

Mrs. Fence, you were made just like the rest of us women, you have to know something is not right. If not, the following questions should help you.

Is he performing the same in bed?

Is he even in your bed or do you sleep in separate beds?

Is he still treating you like the queen that you are?

How about his communication? When was the last time he communicated with you?

When was the last time he made you smile or told you how beautiful you are?

Does he seem nervous when he comes home?

I am trying to help you Mrs. Fence, please work with me. If he could cheat on you right there on your property that is a little too much to swallow. Gather the facts and investigate. By investigating you can ask him, but please know he is not going to tell you the truth. So, if you really want to know, be smart, look and observe. Listen to that little voice inside of you.

Once you have completed your investigation, decide what you would like to do. If you have made the decision, and it is not to stay with him, cut him loose now, while you are young and move on.

Yes you have an eight year old, but what happens if she walks in on her dad one day with the caregiver, or if he brings the caregiver over to the main house while you are away? Imagine the negative impact it will have on her, as a child and a young girl?

If you decide to stay with him, ask God to give you grace and guide your footsteps, so that you will learn to trust again and not continuously hold it against him. That will not be good for anyone in your household.

The one time, God has given us permission to divorce is once your spouse has committed adultery, so do not be afraid to take that route, if that is the one that will bring you peace and happiness. As he is successful, do not feel guilty to claim what you both have built for your family. He should have thought about the consequences of his actions.

May you seek God's guidance as you try to put your family together or if necessary move on. I pray for you that whatever decision you make, you will be at peace with it.

Mr. Fence, if you are reading this book, I hope you repent and make it right with your family and with God. If you do not, please know there is a special place in "hell" just for you.

CHAPTER V

MR. & MRS. PERFECT

Told to me by Mrs. Perfect – Hispanics

Mr. & Mrs. Perfect have been married for approximately 12 years and have three beautiful children; (two boys and a girl, ranging from the ages of four to ten. Mr. & Mrs. Perfect are both Corporate workers and in addition, own a trucking family business.

Mr. & Mrs. Perfect are very adorable and they with their three beautiful children are admired by all. Little do you know Mrs. Perfect, "everything that appears to be perfect, is not necessarily perfect."

Both Mr. & Mrs. Perfect had affairs, while they were dating and eventually broke up but were reunited. Shortly thereafter, they married and moved to California to further their career goals and objectives.

It was during this relocation that Mr. Perfect met someone from his past and rekindled the relationship. Mrs. Perfect, of course, was unaware. The Perfect's moved back to Miami and are still living in Miami today with their three beautiful children. However, so did the "blast" from the past.

Mr. Perfect was required to work late hours sometimes. However, we will later find out that he used this opportunity to his advantage and engaged in extra-curricular activities that were unrelated to work. Readers, you know exactly what I am referring to.

Sometimes, during those supposedly late hours, Mrs. Perfect would ask if he wants her to stop by as they lived very close to his dad and he could baby sit. Mr. Perfect rejected the idea. Someone else was going to be on-site and Mrs. Perfect will only get in the way.

Despite the unknown, Mr. & Mrs. Perfect appeared to be a happy couple and the kids seemed to be happy and well adjusted; then one day, Mr. Perfect told Mrs. Perfect, "I think we should take some time away from each other, but it is not because of another woman, I just need my space." How did I become privy to this? I was on my way to work and I stopped for fuel.

Mrs. Perfect was at the same gas station filling up her tank and when I went by to say hello and asked how she was doing, she began to cry uncontrollably. I realized something was wrong and at the same time, I noticed there was a little café near by, so I told her to park her car by the station, and if she had time, we could have some coffee at the near by café.

She agreed and drove with me to the café, so we could converse privately as she composed herself. Lucky for both of us, we worked close by within 10-15 minutes away in the same area.

We arrived at the café and I tried to console Mrs. Perfect. It took some time, but she finally calmed down and proceeded to tell me that things are really bad in their marriage and she does not know why. I asked her if Mr. Perfect was cheating and she told me he was not and that he said "it was not because of another woman, he just did not want to be married any more."

All the while, I am internalizing, "Mrs. Perfect, wake up, please and smell the coffee." She advised me that she does not believe that he is cheating, since he also told her, he would like a divorce because he does not want to cheat on her. I think he meant to say, he did not want to continue cheating. Guess, he probably felt guilty.

I told Mrs. Perfect what Mr. Perfect said does not make any sense. Why would he give up his beautiful family to be single? When did he discovered that he did not want to be married and wanted to go chill at his dad's house?

In addition, I advised her that my belief is that there is another woman in the picture and that is why he is leaving. She did not want to hear that and insisted that he is not cheating on her. Everyone has to find that place where they can be comforted and most of the time, it is to live in denial, because the alternative is too painful.

Throughout the next couple of months, every time I called to check on Mrs. Perfect, she would begin to cry and continued to let me know that things were really bad between them. She reminded me that Mr. Perfect insisted that he wants out of the marriage and that he is no longer in love with her.

From that point on, I limited the calling and waited for her to call me when she wanted to converse. I reassured her that I will always be here for her and she could call me at any time. Subsequently, each time I saw her, she would burst into tears, or I would notice that she was crying.

I too, cried internally for her. No one should have to go through so much pain. I knew she was at her wits end and I gave her lots of hugs and did my best to cheer her up and pull her out of that frame of thought. Try as you might, sometimes you cannot help in that moment, only the spouse can.

The pain I saw in Mrs. Perfect eyes seemed insurmountable and I could only imagine how she felt. I told her to hang in there and to continue to pray, knowing that "God changes things" and the "effectual fervent prayer of a righteous man and/ or woman availeth much."

She told me that every day she woke up, she cried and cried. My heart was crying for her and for those three children that needed both of their parents. What is wrong with our men? Are they so dense, that they cannot see straight and understand the pain and hurt they inflict on someone they are suppose to care about or promised to love?

I met with Mrs. Perfect several times and we talked for hours and hours. I also invited her to my home, so she could get a break from her surroundings. Mrs. Perfect is a woman of God and has strong Christian and family values. She told me she was going to grant Mr. Perfect the divorce. My response to her was "do you love your husband?" She answered "yes." At which time I said to her, "if you love your husband, whatever you do, do not give him a divorce, fight for your marriage."

I told her "please do not make it easy for him." He is looking for an easy way out and is using her kind spirit to get it. She told me that she was torn apart as she asked me "how do you fight for someone that does not love you or want to be with you any more?" In addition, she mentioned "the pain is unbearable and I love him so much but it is painful hearing those words, that he does not love me any more; it is excruciating."

I further advised Mrs. Perfect "your husband does not know what he wants at this time. He is going through a phase and thinks there is something better out there." In addition, I told her he is having a moment and feels like he wants to be single, "you have to save him from himself."

The Devil is continuously tempting our men and women of God and as spouses we have to be strong and not be so easily swayed to give in and let them have their lustful desires. We have to stop the epidemic that has taken over our country and this world.

In addition, I reiterated to Mrs. Perfect that "even if you no longer love him, do not make it easy for him, by giving him what he wants, make it difficult for him." Yes, as a Christian, I told her that.

Why should any one make it easy on someone who has tremendously hurt them and wants to discard their marriage like yesterday's news? It is not over until we the wives say it is over. I repeat myself it is not over until we say that it is over and God says it is over. Men, remember this, you think you are in control, but you are not, God is.

Mrs. Perfect hung in there and experienced so much pain and heartache but I continued to pray for her and encouraged her to stay in prayer, for prayer changes things. Never underestimate the power of prayer and the mighty God that we serve. "He is able to do all things, exceedingly more than we can even ask or think." We just have to believe, even when it seems hopeless.

Time went by and the days, nights, weeks, months were lonely ones for Mrs. Perfect. Mr. Perfect was still at home, (sleeping on the couch) but his mind, heart and soul were not there, just his body. Some women might ask what else is needed.

A friend once told me, that "having a man at home, even though he is only physically there, is better than not having a man." What do you say to that? Are you kidding me? Are you so desperate for a man and have such low self-esteem that you would settle for a cheating couch potato?

Through out all of this time, Mrs. Perfect still maintained Mr. Perfect, was indeed "Mr. Perfect", and that he was not cheating. I, however, believed with everything in me that he was, but I did not push that on her, as I did not want to add to her burden and emotional state.

I am a firm believer that whatever is done in secret, will eventually be brought to light. It may not be tomorrow, next week, next month or next year, but it will be brought to light.

One evening, Mrs. Perfect attended a social event in Key West and Mr. Perfect also had a social event supposedly in Palm Beach, that same day, relative to his work, (so he said). It was at Mrs. Perfect's event that she received a text message from Mr. Perfect, advising her that he had packed and moved to his father's house. This is every woman's nightmare.

What a coward! Could not even respectfully, tell her face to face, but waited until she was out of the house, packed his things, moved out and then sent her a text. Is this what marriages have to endure? Are there no values to the vows we have taken?

The children were with their grandparents during this time. Now, it will be up to Mrs. Perfect to face those young faces and tell all three of them that their dad will not be living at home for a while.

Imagine leaving your house, going to an event and then returning home to an empty house because your spouse cowardly left while you were gone. This is due for primetime. Keep in mind, all this time, Mrs. Perfect is still saying that Mr. Perfect is not cheating.

She mentioned "it is not his style." What really is a man's style? I just know I will have to be there for Mrs. Perfect when she realizes that he has been cheating and is still cheating, which is why he wanted to move out. Her world is going to be crushed.

On the way home, Mrs. Perfect, finally became not so "perfect". She called Mr. "Imperfect" and initially told him that he will be the one telling their children, what he has done and is doing. However, being the kind hearted person that she is she reconsidered and compromised for the children's sake and agreed that they will tell them together.

The time came and they eventually told their children what was going on and that daddy will not be living there any more. They reassured them that both mommy and daddy loved them and it is not their fault that daddy is no longer there. You know the rest, the usual "blah, blah, and blah."

Weeks and months went by and the children were shuffled between both parents and occasionally they all got together for family gatherings, for the sake of the children, as they tried to maintain some type of normalcy in their lives. During this time, Mr. Perfect was very uncouth with Mrs. Perfect, but she still maintained there was no other lady in his life. I internalized what I wanted to say at that point but said nothing as I realized she could not handle it.

How we can be in such denial sometimes is a mystery. I guess we have to do what is necessary to protect our hearts and minds. Mrs. Perfect continued to hold on and hold on to her belief that Mr. Perfect was not cheating. No, not her Mr. Perfect!

Both Mr. & Mrs. Perfect attended a social gathering together. Even though they were separated, they still shared the same circle of friends. At this gathering, Mr. Perfect introduced someone as a childhood friend, at which time Mrs. Perfect felt a strange feeling in her gut, but quickly dismissed the notion and would not let her mind take her out of her denial zone.

Mr. & Mrs. Perfect continued to live separate lives but Mrs. Perfect told me that he had started coming around more often and staying longer hours, when he would pick up and drop off the children and that she was continuing to pray but she was not going to give in to a divorce. (This was a very wise decision).

Again, all this time, Mr. Perfect maintained that he was not seeing anyone and Mrs. Perfect continued to believe him. We all have the tendency to believe whatever makes us feel safe. We find it easy at times to believe it is happening to another couple, but no, not to us.

Mr. Perfect took a business trip to California and after arriving back at the Miami Airport in the Cab to his dad's house, they were hit with a truck, coming from an intersection. Mr. Perfect and the other passenger in the car were injured and taken to the nearest hospital for treatment.

The other passenger being the mistress was released but Mr. Perfect was hospitalized for two weeks and Mrs. Perfect never left his side. The mistress however, did not call nor visit Mr. Perfect. It never ceases to astound me. We always have to pick up the pieces of those who have wronged us. I am reminded of the movie "a diary of a mad black woman".

Where are the mistresses when you need them? Of course they disappear. They did not promise in the sight of God to love you, honor you, forsaking all others, till death do us part. Where are they? Can you find them? No you cannot. They have left the building.

Are you surprised? Well, don't be. They certainly did not sign up to comfort you when you are sick and in pain. They did not sign up to be by your side when you cannot sleep at night. They did not sign up to cook you chicken soup when you have the flu or pour you a glass of water to take with an aspirin when you have a headache. They signed up for a "well" man not a "sick" one. You are of no value to them in your time of need.

Simply speaking, the only thing they promised you is to give you a release when you need one or when they need one. Foolish men, I thought you knew this. Can't you tell? Deep down, no matter how much a woman tells you she loves you in the moment, she knows if you are married and you are cheating on your wife, what will prevent you from doing the same to her?

While Mr. Perfect was hospitalized, he had time to reflect on what he had done to his family and during one of his wife's visit, he told her that he was sorry for walking out on them and pleaded with her to forgive him. I would say, his confession was a "limited edition" version, as he did not come clean with every thing.

Listen up, men, if you wrong a woman, the confession is not valid unless you provide full disclosure, which means do not leave anything out or conveniently forget something. What is not important to you, it is important to your spouse. Furthermore, as women, we know when you are not giving us the full details.

When the time came for Mr. Perfect to be discharged from the hospital, Mrs. Perfect was there to pick him up. She told him that she had forgiven him and that it was ok to come home, providing that he would agree to counseling, to which he did.

After they reached home, he sat down with his family, apologized for his behavior and told them he was home to stay. The following week, Mr. & Mrs. Perfect sought counseling and began the long road ahead of trying to rebuild their marriage. It is amazing what counseling can do.

No wonder, most men do not like to entertain the idea of counseling. They know the effects it could have on them. Unless they are willing to confess it all, they cannot handle it, therefore, they would prefer not to attend. Not attending, however, does not make the problem go away.

For Mr. Perfect, he realized that failing to attend was not an option. Therefore, they continued to attend the counseling sessions and about six weeks into counseling, Mr. Perfect was consumed by infidelity guilt, and finally admitted to Mrs. Perfect, that he had an affair with the childhood friend (the same one he introduced at the social gathering).

He further admitted that this childhood friend was the reason why he left his family but he promised that he was no longer seeing her. In addition, he stated that he was in a bad place at the time and he began crying. He cried and cried like a baby asking Mrs. Perfect to forgive him.

Ladies, always use your God-given intuition. Remember, Mrs. Perfect felt something in her gut when she was introduced to her but she dismissed it. Never dismiss or ignore your feelings. That is why we are the way we are. We can spot a phony from a mile away.

Please do not doubt yourselves and believe the nonsense that spouses try to get over on us. We know better. Do not let them play us for fools. They are foolish if they think that we are oblivious to our surroundings. Don't they know that before we ask them a question, we know the answer? We only ask, so they can "hang" themselves.

Mrs. Perfect often travels for her job 50% of the time and she later learned that it was during those times while she was away, Mr. Perfect invited the mistress over to the house for sexual escapades, in their bed, while the kids were sleeping. Can you imagine the emotional turmoil that Mrs. Perfect is facing as she is being told this? Can you imagine? What would you do? What should Mrs. Perfect do?

Most of us can think of many options we could take. Some of them would be legal and some of them not so legal. Mr. Perfect, I do not think you would want to find out the illegal actions one can take against cheating spouses.

Help me to understand this. You will bring a woman in my bed, in my place of comfort, really? Are you out of your mind? Do you not value anything that we share and have shared, or are you so desperate, you have to have it and the best place is in your wife's bed?

Come on guys, you have to do better than this. How can you think it is ok to bring someone in your spouse's home, more so in the bed you share with her as husband and wife? How can you totally disrespect your home especially while your children are in the other room sleeping?

What if your wife comes home to surprise you? What if the children wake up? Who knows, they probably did at some point. Oops! I forgot, you do not think, you are absolutely a "dirt bag" to do this.

Let me guess, you are the man of the house and you can do whatever your little brain tells you to do, and it is ok. Well, surprise, surprise, it does not work that way. A wise man once said "you make your choices but you do not choose your consequences."

As Mrs. Perfect and I continued to speak on a regular basis, one day we were having a very friendly conversation and doing some catch-up from the last time we spoke. It was during this time that she informed me that I was right all along, that Mr. Perfect was indeed having an affair and she told me all the details that she had found out.

I listened and I did not say to her "I told you so". She did however advised me that she sometimes feel like divorcing him and at times, she wants to continue to work on their marriage.

I certainly can understand that at times she wants to divorce him. For me, every time I would have to go in that bed or think about that bed, I would want to hurt him badly. Your bedroom is the most sacred room in the house. It is where you share complete intimacy.

The Bible tells us "marriage is honorable and the bed is undefiled." How dare you men (husbands) bring anyone into our homes and into our beds? Do you get a kick or some sick type of excitement from doing so? Shame on you!

What if it was the other way around? Yes, what if your wife brings someone into your bed? (Ok, some women do). How would you handle and can you handle that? Can you forgive like most women would forgive you? Think about that the next time the thought crosses your mind.

Think about a man being in your bed with your wife while you are really out working at night or travelling on legitimate business, making financial gain for your family, but your spouse is spending time with another man in your home and in your bed.

Think about your children in the other room, you are at work and your wife is going "at it" couple rooms down the hall and I would venture to say really enjoying herself, for after all, it is not a one time, deal. Think if you would be able to share that bed or look at your wife's face and tell her ever again that you love her and want your marriage to work. For once, think men. "Think like a woman but please act like a gentleman!"

Keep in mind the one solace that Mrs. Perfect held on to, was that Mr. Perfect remained faithful in all of this. Therefore, let me tell you what Mrs. Perfect did. Mrs. Perfect had some choice words that as a child of God, I cannot repeat, or include in this book. However, I will give you the condensed version. First, there were the following questions:

Did you enjoy it while she was doing it to you?

Did she enjoy your "itsy, bitsy" spider web?

Were you enough for her or did she demand toys?

Were you thinking of me while you were in my bed with this creature?

Were you laughing at me and saying how silly I am and how you cannot wait to divorce me?

What about our children, did they wake up and you ignored them?

Was the sex all you ever wanted, was it worth it?

How many times did it happen and how many times in one night?

Did you do to her everything you do to me?

Did you get enough of her or do you still want more and how much more?

You should have died in the car accident and I would not have to look at your sorry, ugly, cheating face.

You are nothing but a scum bag and I hope you are hurting hearing me say these words, the way you have hurt me.

I am not sure if I still want to be married to you but I can tell you, anytime this happens again, please leave. Do not tell me about it while you are still in my presence, for anything can happen.

Mrs. Perfect continued and said that she told him "even though we are doing counseling, there is no guarantee I will not change my mind and divorce your sorry", well, fill in the blank. She went on to say that Mr. Perfect basically cried like a baby, a "baby girl", that is. Yes, we can make men cry like little girls. As a matter of fact, I think she said he "bawled". He again asked for forgiveness and said how sorry he was.

She said he was on the floor and she felt like kicking him while he was down there. (I wanted to ask, "why didn't you?") I believe she sensed what I was thinking, as she proceeded to tell me that the only reason she did not do it was because he is her "babies" daddy.

Spouses, you take us to some places that we do not want to go and for what? Please tell me what you think you are experiencing in the "wild" that you cannot have at home? Remember, whatever you are dipping into, you are not the only one. Aren't you concerned about who/what else is participating and dipping? Have a little respect please for yourself. Have some dignity.

I am sure that anyone who has been in this situation, or may go through this situation, similar words were or will be spoken. Yes, Christian or non-Christian. We are human beings and we feel and we hurt. Therefore, to Mrs. Perfect we say "Bravo".

Mrs. Perfect further advised that she took to social media and addressed the mistress's family. She advised them of the type of person the mistress in question is and also demanded the mistress's telephone # from Mr. Perfect. At this time, Mrs. Perfect, immediately contacted the said mistress and told her she is a home-wrecker among other things. Use your imagination.

The mistress's response was that it was never her intent to ruin Mrs. Perfect's family. Can you please tell me, if you are sleeping in my bed with my spouse, what exactly is your objective, if not to ruin my family and take my spouse for yourself? How ignorant are you? Do you have any type of intellect or were you passed over when it was given out? Please examine your ways. You have hurt a family that has done nothing to you, just for a roll in the hay.

Mrs. Perfect is a very good friend of mine and when she hurts, I hurt. For months I had to listen to her and see her in pain and all you have to say is it was not your intent. Mr. Perfect, please do not tell me you were too weak to turn away. You are a married man and you know better. Therefore, much is expected from you. I pray that Mrs. Perfect has indeed forgiven you or finds the strength to do so.

Mistresses, stay away from married men and seek out those who are single. One of the great benefits is you will no longer be called a mistress and you can regain some dignity. If cheating is what you do for a hobby, find another; maybe sky diving or rock climbing. My prayer for you is that you will find the peace and contentment that you are looking for. These can only be found in Christ.

Spouses, as women, we know when and what you are thinking. Yes, we do. Remember our minds work overtime and also remember you do not choose your consequences for your actions. We play a vital part, so always be mindful, prior to being silly.

Keep in mind, that as nice as we are, we do snap at times, so please think before you act. Spend time in God's word, if you are a true man of God and you would not have time to think of the worldly pleasures and the lusts of the flesh. Use that extra energy you found to spice up your love life with your wife instead of with someone else. I am sure your spouse will appreciate it and if she is happy you will be happier. Think about it.

Mrs. Perfect advised me that they are taking one day at a time and not taking each other for granted. Mr. Perfect has renewed his faith in God and they are planning to renew their marriage vows in 2015.

My Advice to Mr. & Mrs. Perfect

Mrs. Perfect, if you are reading this book, and I really hope you are, I applaud your courage and your steadfastness for hanging in there, against all odds. You stood by the one that you love and the one that you told God for better or worse. You are to be commended as some of us may have ended up in prison.

Your bed is the most sacred and precious part of your marriage, as it is where you connect intimately. As previously stated, the Bible says "marriage is honorable and the bed is undefiled." I am very happy to hear that Mr. Perfect is now showering you with the respect, love, romance and commitment that you so richly deserve.

Mr. Perfect, if you are reading this please continue to do the right thing and love on your spouse and your family. You do not deserve Mrs. Perfect, but the God in her has allowed her to give you another chance. I do hope you realize that the distractions out there are not worth it, as you eventually found out. Appreciate the one you were blessed with. Please do not mess-up this opportunity. Treasure the gift of family that God has given you and do not let any negative force destroy what God has joined together. I am sure you have learned your lesson and will not take that route again.

I pray that you will honor Mrs. Perfect and your children and stay committed to Christ. The road is not going to be an easy one, as there are many sharks and fishes in the sea. Please, love on your spouse and not on someone else.

I encourage both of you to continue to receive counseling as long as you need it and do not be ashamed to tell your story. You are no doubt amongst the top percentile of cheating spouses that were given a second chance.

The good thing is you have both won, the mistress did not. God kept you. Continue to pray together and be faithful. Remember, the family that prays together, stays together.

CHAPTER VI

MR. & MRS. MARKERS

Told to me by Mrs. Markers - Europeans

Mr. & Mrs. Markers have been married for approximately three decades and have two grown beautiful children; (a son 24 years of age and a daughter 28). The youngest is still at home and the oldest, the daughter, is married. Mr. & Mrs. Markers own a family construction business and Mrs. Markers works as a Director for a prestigious firm.

The Markers are very successful and they encourage their children to be self employed and pursue their dreams; reassuring them, if they can see it, they can make it a reality. They often remind them that growing up they had nothing but they worked hard as adults and were able to provide a good life for their family.

Mrs. Markers is one of the most elegant ladies you will find. She is poised and soft spoken and will give her last dime or piece of clothing to anyone who needs it. I love Mrs. Markers dearly and we often communicate by telephone.

One Sunday afternoon about three years ago, Mrs. Markers contacted me and told me her suspicions of her spouse's cheating. She said his entire behavior has changed. He rarely converses with her and when he does, it is only a few words.

Mrs. Markers further advised that there is infrequent action in the bedroom and when it occurs, it seems like a "booty call". She said she is frustrated and something has to change as she wants and deserves more from her marriage.

She went on to say that there is no passion, no hugs or kisses, no dining out, not even on special events. In addition, she mentioned that he does not take the time to simply acknowledge her birthday and their anniversary.

My heart was broken for Mrs. Markers. Just listening and feeling the pain in her voice, as she poured her heart out to me was so intense. I asked her if she had any proof that he was being unfaithful to her and she said "no", but as previously said, a woman knows, yes we do. We may be in denial, but deep down, we know. I am sure it is painful to accept but sooner or later it is best that we face reality to avoid enabling this behavior.

Mrs. Markers further said that during holidays and often times on weekends, instead of spending time with her, Mr. Markers leaves in the morning and does not return until night time. She has no idea where he goes and why. She further reiterated that there is no communication and he is indifferent to her advances.

As Mrs. Markers is my friend, I also know Mr. Markers but I had no idea he would be in this category of disappointments. I am totally appalled of this mistrust, and I am hoping it is not true. However, we know if it looks, sounds, and acts like a duck, chances are it is a duck.

Mrs. Markers is a Christian with old fashioned values and she does not believe in divorce. In addition, she is afraid to confront Mr. Markers with her suspicion. I have advised her on several occasions, to be forthright and ask him directly so she can observe his reaction.

During one of our conversations, Mrs. Markers informed me that she aches for her spouse to wine and dine her. She yearns for him to tell her she is beautiful, to converse with her and to be loving and spontaneous.

In addition, Mrs. Markers admits that she yearns to spend quality time with Mr. Markers, talking and romancing the night away. She said "it used to be so magical, just being in each other's presence and in each others arms."

Mrs. Markers pointed out that she does not want a booty call, she wants love and caressing. She longs for the dancing, cuddling, laughter, the attention. She misses his touch in all the right places and because he does not lead she cannot follow.

This is so sad. I wish I could have a conversation with Mr. Markers and plainly ask him, what is his problem? I cannot though, as that will only make the situation worse. In addition, I do not believe in interfering with someone's marriage.

Mrs. Markers advised me that first thing in the morning he goes outside on the patio and talks softly on his cell phone. At night time, it is physically in bed with him, on his heart. It never leaves his side, not even when he goes to the bathroom.

Come on, what is up with the cell phone? Can you at least respectfully wait until you leave the house to make the call, to the whatever, or whoever? It is obvious Mr. Markers has left the marriage and is there in person only, his heart has wondered elsewhere. The Bible tells us "you cannot love two persons at the same time." You will hate one and love the other; you will cling to one and want to be away from the other. Basically, you will despise the other person. In most cases the spouse is the one that is despised.

I am afraid that Mrs. Markers does not realize it, but this is exactly what is happening. He sees Mrs. Markers as a thorn in his side. I can tell you that he is feeling this way because he is "guilty as sin" and he suspects Mrs. Markers knows what he is doing, even though she has not voiced it.

One of Mrs. Markers' friends told her that she was privy to seeing Mr. Marker "chasing" a young lady while driving. Does Mr. Markers think he is 18 years old? It is astounding how the older men desire to revert to their teenage years, forgetting those years are gone, never to be returned. Please grow up.

Marriage is a lifetime commitment, and both men and women need to wise up and live up to the oath taken, in the sight of God, family and friends. What are you chasing out there, when you have everything you should desire right at your finger tips? Get a "grip", please. Stop chasing 20% on the street corners, when you have 100% at home.

Mrs. Markers said that she is contemplating what to do. She continues to crave for intimacy with her husband, the way it used to be. Despite it all she still does everything for him; clean, cook, wash, and how does he repay her? He repays her by actually sleeping with someone else.

I am a firm believer if you are sleeping with someone other than your spouse, then please leave and be with that person. How could you be living at home with your spouse expecting her to be domesticated and you continuously ignore her. Mrs. Markers also said that at times, when he does get close, his breath has an unfamiliar scent. I wonder why?

As previously stated, if it acts, walks, quacks and let me add "smells" like a duck, it is a duck and has been in the "dirty pond" waters where many, others have been. Mr. Markers, why? You have one of the most attractive ladies on the planet who adores you.

Mrs. Markers made reference that one time they were traveling together and she was the driver. Her telephone rang and she asked him to get it for her and he silently refused. She said he did not flinch but simply pretended she was not there. It was like she was conversing with her self. That is the uttermost disrespect.

Could it be that he knows when his cell phone rings, it is a "mistress" calling, so he is probably thinking the same and wants to pass the blame on to Mrs. Markers? We know that a guilty conscience does not need an accuser.

Readers, as previously stated, Mrs. Markers is one of the most attractive ladies you would find and she has everything going for her, except the "loser" of a husband. Yes, in my opinion, everyone that cheats is more often than not, a "loser". Therefore, Mrs. Markers, you need to get tough and confront Mr. Markers.

More than likely, Mr. Markers is not going to come clean, but you can at least, know that you asked the question. You then can observe and move on. You are your own woman and do not need a man, just to be in the house and not communicate. As you said, you have more conversation with the television than with Mr. Markers. This is funny and sad at the same time.

Mrs. Makers also told me that Mr. Markers often travel overseas and is sometimes away for two or three consecutive days. Unfortunately, he has never asked her to accompany him, so they can enjoy the sceneries and make new memories. Could it be those trips are for pleasure instead of business and someone else accompanies him? What do you think? "Who cheats more than a Politician?"

I suggested that Mrs. Markers inform him that she would like to travel along and explore all the beautiful things he is fortunate to enjoy. She is however, afraid to ask in the event, he says no, it will be too painful for her to endure. You would think that any loving husband would make the offer, and the wife would not have to ask.

Mrs. Markers advised me that many times she invites him to attend Church but he continues to refuse. She said it has been almost two years he has not attended. This is a man that used to be a deacon in the Church. Well, ok, let us keep in mind, recently, a "deacon" walked into the church and shot the preacher. Surprise, surprise, the church is not exempt, and that includes from the head to the tail.

I cannot stress enough, that this cheating behavior has become an epidemic across the country and we need to do something about it. If you are not ready for marriage, just do not get married and you will not have to give an account to anyone, at least no earthly one, just your Creator.

Remember, with Him, he already knows what you are doing, so you cannot lie to Him. Before you cheat, He knows your desires and your plans.

Yes, God sees all and knows all. I think if most people realize this, they will seek to do the right thing, at all times.

Please do not quote the scripture that says "even though I seek to do good evil is present with me". You know exactly what you are doing, and what you desire to do, so stop using the scriptures to excuse your behavior. Remember His word says, that "a child of God cannot continue in sin."

My Advice to Mr. & Mrs. Markers

Mr. Markers, what you are doing to Mrs. Markers is not right. You are married and should therefore conduct your self in that manner. There should not be any secrets between you and your spouse.

Why the secret phone calls? Why don't you take time out and appreciate your wife? Make her feel special. Whatever you may have going on out there, is it really worth it? If you were to get sick, who will be by your side? What did Mrs. Markers do to deserve this betrayal?

As a Christian, do you not read the Bible and understand what it means when it says "all adulterers will have their place in hell?" Do you believe all the other sections of the Bible except the scriptures pertaining to adultery? Be wise and correct your actions. Ask Mrs. Markers to forgive you and hope that she does. You may then go to God and repent of your wrong doings.

Mrs. Markers, it seems that Mr. Markers is taking you for granted, as you have been married for quite sometime. He knows you have a good heart and feels that you will not leave him. That is true and you do not have to leave, but at the same time, you do not have to tolerate that type of behavior in your own home.

My friend, you are a wise woman. You know he is cheating on you. What are you going to do about it? First of all confront him and be strong in doing so. Do not be intimated. Get him to confess, once he does this, let him wait for at least a month before you let him know if you are going to forgive him and stay married.

He is caught with his hands in the cookie jar and you need to let him squirm for a little bit. Let him realize how close he came to losing you and will lose you if this continues. Remember, when you see anyone on television in this type of situation, you always say, "put him out," so why don't you take a page from your playbook and do the same. Do not be afraid.

Let him see what it is to be alone and to see if the "so-called" mistress will take him in. I can almost guarantee you that she will not; as I am sure she has others that she sees in addition to him. Men, are you really into the mistresses that you will be willing to leave your spouses, all for sex?

You need to realize that most of the time it is all about what they can get from you and not what they can give to you. You are just another man to them after all, you are someone's husband. Are you so obscure that you literally cannot see the forest from the trees? Ok, you are blinded by the temporary feel good "one-minute" situation.

Anyone disagrees? The funny thing, most of the one-minute ventures leave you still hungry and you come home, rush in the shower and want your spouse to "roll over" after you just "rolled off". Women, please say no to those spouses, during those times, if you are observant as to what is going on.

Mrs. Markers should you decide to forgive Mr. Markers, please let him know your demands and how you would like to be treated and appreciated. Do not settle for anything but the best. You have earned it and it is well-deserving. Remind him that there is always a "ram in the bushes" and you can grab that "ram", if you so desire.

I repeat, if you need to grab the "ram" from the bushes, you have the right to do so, based on God's word, as Mr. Markers, strayed from the marriage and defiled your bed. Let him see and know that you do not have to settle and you do not intend to settle. Let him work to earn your respect and trust all over again.

My hope for you however, is that you remain together and be faithful and loyal moving forward. You have spent many years together and that speaks volume. The road ahead is not going to be easy but with God all things are possible. As your friend, always feel free to reach out to me. Remember, I am only a phone call away.

CHAPTER VII

MR. & MRS. WONDERFUL

Told to me by Mrs. Wonderful – Barbadians

Mr. & Mrs. Wonderful are indeed wonderful and have been married for approximately 23 years. They have three beautiful children; (two girls and a boy ranging from the ages of 14 - 22). Mr. & Mrs. Wonderful are indeed wonderful. Mrs. Wonderful is a born leader and has been self employed for quite some time. Mr. Wonderful has had a few struggles but is now a senior manager in Corporate America.

Mrs. Wonderful is a beautiful petite Barbadian and we have been known to be mistaken for sisters on several occasions, even by our own families. Mrs. Wonderful is the bread winner of the family and there were times when it was tough on Mr. Wonderful as he was trying to find meaningful employment. Mrs. Wonderful told me that she believed he was cheating on her because he had plenty of free time due to unemployment but was never accessible by telephone. Please know the Devil always finds mischief for idle hands to be engaged.

It was during these times that Mrs. Wonderful advised me that she sought comfort from her first love. She mentioned that Mr. Wonderful went through a series of jobs and the last one he found, he was excited and stuck with it until they brought in a young man freshly out of college to be his superior. He was very unhappy about that and eventually quit. Who quits a job when there is a family to support?

The financial strain was overwhelming and again fell on Mrs. Wonderful. As a result, bitterness surfaced on both sides. She said love making was out of the question. No surprise there, as you know, for most women, if things are not right, we cannot indulge, sorry! As time went by, the bitterness and unhappy times escalated and Mrs. Wonderful could not stand being in the same room with him.

Mrs. Wonderful told me she advised Mr. Wonderful, that she was traveling to Jamaica for a few days as she needed to get away. Mr. Wonderful did not protest. Funny that is. He was doing his own thing as well and Mrs. Wonderful will eventually find out. It is all about confession but who will be the first to confess?

The weekend came and Mrs. Wonderful packed and flew to Jamaica, where she connected with her first love and did what she felt she had to do. Mrs. wonderful said to me after she got back. "It was the best time of my life."

She further said "I do not remember the last time I felt loved and wanted, like he made me felt." "You may say it was wrong and I know it was but it felt so right." She also asked "why should I be miserable when I can find the happiness I richly deserve?"

As she continued to speak about the amazing time she had, I could see the joy in her face and the love she felt for this man, while she continued telling me about the weekend she enjoyed. She stated that "it was so beautiful over there, the long walks on the beach and the tour of the island, sitting next to him, while he cuddled me, was just heavenly".

In addition, she said, "I love my husband but I have no regrets in what I did, and if I have to do it again, I will." She continued, "my dear friend you may say you cannot love two men at the same time, but I disagree. You can just different levels of love and different types of love." Mrs. Wonderful also stated "please do not condemn me as you are not in my shoes, and you do not know what you would do until you are faced with my situation."

Guess what Mrs. Wonderful, you may be right that no one knows what he/she will do if faced with this situation. It is all about the people involved and where you are spiritually at the time. One thing for sure is that one of them will definitely be hurt and it is usually the spouse. The lover has no ties to you, but your spouse does. Bottom line, you have to know what is best for you and who you would like to spend your time with but you cannot have both. I further advised her that no matter how she justified it, as a married woman, what she did was wrong.

Mrs. Wonderful admitted to me that as the months and years went by, she continued to yearn for this man and wanted to meet up with him again, but the God in her did not allow her to do that. She kept feeling guilty and thinking about what example she would be setting for her children.

She knew some things only come by praying and fasting, and this was definitely one of them. It was a tough road ahead but she hung in there with her spouse. He finally landed a job as manager for a prestigious firm in Miami, and he is now a senior manager.

As time went by, the guilt consumed Mrs. Wonderful and she knew in order for their marriage to work, she would have to confess. It was not easy for her but she looked within herself and found the strength and courage needed. She then confessed to Mr. Wonderful that she had an affair with her first love and she explained to him why she did it.

Women are definitely brave. Whatever we do, we eventually own up to it. Not men, even if you see them doing it, they will tell you it is not so. Sometimes it does seem as though they are from another planet. They will do everything in their power to convince you it is not what you think.

Mrs. Wonderful was very forthcoming with Mr. Wonderful and made mention of the unhappiness and bitterness she felt towards him when he quit his job and put all the strain back in her lap. She pointed out to him, the lack of communication that took place as he was making decisions without consulting with her, especially one that will affect their financial status. She demanded that he listens to her concerns and takes her seriously as her patience was wearing "thin".

Additionally, she said that despite Mr. Wonderful not being attentive to her and not effectively communicating, she realized that he was still a great man, father and husband. Mr. Wonderful in hearing his spouse's confession was moved. He did not judge her or yelled at her. He held her close and told her he was sorry that his lack of attention and communication, led to her infidelity. He is indeed a wonderful man!

In addition, Mr. Wonderful ceased that moment and confessed that about eight years into their marriage, he had a "one-night" stand and he was now asking her to forgive him.

I could not believe it as she was telling me this but at the same time, I was glad he had the courage to come clean. Are there any men or women left that are not cheating?

Mr. Wonderful then proceeded to inform Mrs. Wonderful that throughout the years he became withdrawn because of the guilt he felt for what he had done. He admitted he did not know how to tell her, for fear of her leaving. Confession is good for the soul!

This is truly an amazing couple. They confessed to each other and to God and asked for his forgiveness and for him to give them strength to move forward with their family, the way it was meant to be. This is the way it should be. Acknowledge that you have wronged each other and make it right.

Mr. & Mrs. Wonderful are living their dream and they are enjoying each other. Mrs. Wonderful's business is blooming and Mr. Wonderful still has his job as a senior manager. They have become very successful and it is nice to know that they can share that success with each other. They both made mistakes but their love for each other sustained their marriage.

Although they are extremely busy, they find time for each other and they engage in family worship. What a blessing when a family has gone through hell and back and can share their story to be uplifting to other families.

Please keep in mind, whatever you are going through, someone is going through something more challenging or has already experienced something similar, so hang in there! Mr. & Mrs. Wonderful did all that and now all is well in their household.

Every now and again, Mrs. Wonderful calls me and her tone radiates as she talks about Mr. Wonderful and how their marriage has turned around and they are in a good place. There is nothing too hard for the Lord to do.

My Advice to Mr. & Mrs. Wonderful

Keep doing what you are doing. Put God first in your lives and do not look back at the past but look forward towards the future. What you have gone through seems to have made you stronger. Please keep the communication line open and do not be quick to get angry and accusatory.

Be kind and loving to each other. Spend quality time together and do not take each other for granted. Be an example, so that your children will follow in your footsteps, as you follow in the footsteps of the Lord. Know that you will experience many challenges, but you can face whatever life throws at you, together.

Mrs. Wonderful, you are indeed a wonderful person. You fell short and had a moment, so you had to do what you felt you needed to do. Should you however, get the urge to be with your first love, put that energy and passion into Mr. Wonderful and soon that first love will be nothing but a fleeting memory.

I encourage you to keep in mind there is a reason why your spouse's name is Mr. Wonderful, and why you married him. Do not be afraid to share your innermost feelings and desires with him. That is why you have each other.

You are one as Christ is one with the Church, so please do not hold back. Do not give him a reason to look elsewhere; even though if we are truthful, they do not need a reason. If they are going to cheat, they will cheat.

I know I may seem contradictory to my own advice, but you understand that when you said I do, it was for better or worse. I know you never imagined the worse will come so soon, but it did. The good thing is however, it seems like your storm has passed.

Therefore, take comfort in knowing that the same God who saw you through is still with you. Be steadfast in your faith and in your marriage knowing that the best is yet to come.

Chapter VIII

MR. & MRS. LYER

<u>Told to me by Mr. Lyer's Sister - Americans</u>

Mr. & Mrs. Lyer are an interesting family in the community. Mr. Lyer works as a pest control supervisor and Mrs. Lyer works as a director within a Fortune 500 Company. Married for 27 years, they have four children; three boys and one girl, ranging from ages 18 to 24. Mr. & Mrs. Lyer are admired by all, but little do they know what actually goes on in that house of horrors.

Now, do not get me wrong, things were good at the beginning but then everything went sour with Mr. Lyer's out of control cheating behavior. Mr. Lyer's sister said to me, "this is my brother but I have to tell someone what is going on in that family and you are that person."

Mr. Lyer apparently has a cheating problem like an alcoholic has a drinking problem. For the first five years, things seemed to be working fine then it began to spiral when Mrs. Lyer went out of town on a family emergency. Mr. Lyer was left at home and he started by cheating with the neighbor who was just seventeen years of age.

Mr. Lyer's sister mentioned that she is not surprised, as her brother has been sexually active from about ten years of age. At which time he was having sex with 12 and 13 year old girls. In addition, she further said that she does not understand how he gets away with it and what women find attractive in him, as he is only 5' 7" tall and has a "beer" belly. She further said he can be very charming. Maybe that is what is appealing.

For many years, said Mr. Lyer's sister, "my brother has been having affairs with multiple women. Mrs. Lyer, however, was engulfed with her work that she missed what was going on in front and behind of her, until she started to find the condoms used and unused in her husbands pockets and in the trash can".

Per Mr. Lyer's sister, Mrs. Lyer confided in her that they do not use protection therefore, he had to be seeing someone else and also that person or persons had to have been in their home. She further said that Mrs. Lyer decided that she needed to know so she did what she did not realize she could.

Mrs. Lyer confronted her spouse about the condoms and he apparently told her "oh, it is my friend's condom that he asked me to hold for him and sometimes he plays jokes on me by slipping them in my pocket without me knowing."

Mrs. Lyer do you believe such a lie or are you in denial? What about the used ones, how did they get in your trash can? You need to be saying to Mr. Lyer "liar, liar, pants on fire!" Please tell me you are not falling for this. Wake up, the coffee is brewing.

I envision it is difficult to face the truth, because you would need to act and maybe you are not ready to take action. Mr. Lyer's sister continued to tell me more. "My brother has taken several trips within the year without taking Mrs. Lyer and he gives her the excuse that they are business trips." She further stated that there were times he would leave home as early as 6:00am but his job does not start until 9:00am. In addition, he lives about ten minutes away from his job.

His sister continued by saying that she tried to warn her sister-in-law several times but she refused to listen. You would think that after finding the condoms she would be convinced. It is at times easier to believe anything but the truth. His sister pleaded with me to speak with Mrs. Lyer.

I told her that I do not practice getting involved in marital situations. She, however, was not hearing or listening and this is where it got very interesting. She told me to follow Mr. Lyer from his place of employment and see what happens.

I have to admit I was tempted to, but I will not follow my spouse if I suspect he is cheating, therefore, I will not be following anyone's spouse. I do not have the time, the energy nor have I lost my mind. Therefore, I told her I decline.

She went on to tell me that every day when her brother ended work, he visited his main mistress and stayed until about 9:30pm and then went home and told his spouse that he had worked late. It is her belief that they even have a child together, as Mrs. Lyer found a baby bottle in his car, and they do not have a baby.

This is a little overwhelming for me, so I asked if we can convene this conversation at another time. I asked myself if my spouse is doing this to me, will I want to know about it and I believe the answer is yes. We all want to know if the person we love has wronged us. Though it may be difficult to absorb, we need to know. However, we have to proceed with "kid gloves" depending on the person and the situation.

The next time I spoke to Mr. Lyer's sister, it was about a week later and this time she was in tears. She said she knows it is her brother, but what he is doing to his spouse is not right and she really needs my help to get through to her sister-in-law. My heart was heavy and I knew I had to do something.

Mrs. Lyer and I had not spoken in quite sometime as I am aware that her spouse likes to flirt with women, so I avoid those types of situations. Nonetheless, I invited Mrs. Lyer for breakfast and she accepted. At breakfast, to my surprise, she began to unburden all these feelings and told me she needed my opinion on some things that were happening in her life.

Could you imagine? Here I am trying to cautiously speak with her and she is so happy to talk to someone, in so much that she breaks down crying. Things that her sister-in-law thought she was oblivious to, she was not. She has had to bear all these feelings internally for so long. I am so happy that she did not lose her mind, knowing what she knew and feeling what she felt.

Mrs. Lyer confided in me that she has suspected her husband of cheating for many, many years, even before the condom discovery. She shared with me that one day when she returned from visiting her family, she noticed that the family picture was removed from the centerpiece and placed on top of the refrigerator.

She asked Mr. Lyer at the time why did he move the picture. He did not answer. She further stated that on the refrigerator, there was also a porn video. What type of sick twisted episode was taking place in her absence?

Mrs. Lyer said they do not watch porn. Around this time she found an electric toothbrush in her car on the passenger side on the floor. She asked herself what gives, as her spouse does not even know what an electric toothbrush looks like and he definitely will not go to the store to buy one.

Furthermore, why would his toothbrush be in the car? I am crying internally for Mrs. Lyer as she is confiding all this information to me. The audacity for your spouse to bring someone in your home, just like Mr. Perfect did, is like a marriage "crime". It is a "no, no". Men, STOP, and please consider what you are doing, before you proceed.

Why don't you take the tramp on the street where she belongs or behind the garbage bin? Take her to your friend's house, go to her house, please take her anywhere, a dirt road, both of you being dirt bags, but to your spouse's home? Really, then, your spouse is not responsible for what she does, should she find out. Again, I repeat, your spouse is not responsible for what happens next. Are you acquainted with the television show "Snapped"? Just asking...

Spouse, I believe you should know me by now. Therefore, if you are thinking of bringing or have already brought someone to my bed, in my home, please pray that I do not find out, or that I do not realize, that is your plan. So basically, do not even think about it.

The infidelity continues. Another time, Mrs. Lyer said she found female underwear in her brand new bed and also among his clothes when she was folding them, hot from the dryer. Imagine you just washed your husband's mistress' dirty underwear. How revolting and nauseating!

She continued that it got worse over the last three years, when she started receiving text messages from women telling her about them being with her husband. Instead of her husband comforting her, he began finding ways to blame her. She said that he even had the nerve to deny that he had anything to do with these women and that they were making it up?

Mr. Lyer, are you telling me that of all the women in the world, Mrs. Lyer was selected to be told by these women, something that is not true about you? You are lying, Mr. Lyer. No one believes you, so please come clean with Mrs. Lyer. You owe her that much.

This is unreal and Mr. Lyer if you are reading this book, you also have a very special place in "hell". You should be very ashamed of yourself. Mrs. Lyer, at this time, was becoming frantic again and said to me, "if he does not stop the cheating, I will send both him and his mistress to "hell," since they want to be together, they could be together in hell." What do I say to that? Men at times push women to the limit and they snap.

I really tried to calm Mrs. Lyer down and told her that he is not worth it to get herself in trouble with the law. If he does not want to change, she must let him go, just kick him out of her house and move on with her life, but also pray for him. This too, is easier said than done.

The most disgusting part of it all, Mrs. Lyer then showed me unscrupulous pictures that she took from his cell phone. Never in my lifetime, do I want to be a witness to those types of pictures. Not good for me, not good for anyone.

Mr. Lyer was apparently walking around with his mistress's picture and her body parts on his phone. She said when she confronted him, he lied and told her he did not take them and they are not what she thinks. Readers, I know you are not buying into this. "Who cheats more than a Politician?"

I feel Mrs. Lyer's pain all over again. Just repeating this and remembering the turmoil I saw in her countenance is unnerving. Mr. Lyer what kind of sick perverted person are you, to do this to your spouse? What has she ever done to you?

I asked Mrs. Lyer how she discovered the pictures and she told me for days and weeks she did not see his cell phone, which meant he was hiding it from her. Why would your spouse literally hide his cell phone from you?

She became suspicious and started to search for the cell phone. She told me that she found it on top of one of the cabinets. To obtain it she had to climb up on a stool. When a woman is on a mission, she sure accomplishes her goal. Women, we would have done the same.

Mrs. Lyer further said that one Saturday afternoon while Mr. Lyer was sleeping she decided to again search for the phone and she found it. There were three missed calls and there were text messages from the same cell phone number. In addition, she said the said cell phone rang, she answered it and there was music playing but no one spoke.

Being curious, she decided to check the picture gallery, (that is what I would have done as well) and there to her surprise were naked pictures of a woman and her body parts, in a variety of photos/poses, along with what appeared to be one of Mr. Lyer's body parts. Mrs. Lyer said she was torn in millions of tiny pieces inside but she kept it together.

For me it was very painful to listen to and it is painful writing about it. Who wants their spouse to be to that extreme level of deceit and disrespect? She went on to say that she brought the phone to Mr. Lyer and that is when she broke down, showed him the pictures and he said to her, "it is not what you think." What a "dog of a man!" She told me she could not stop crying and for that entire week, she said she cried, cried and cried!

Readers, we are getting to the good part. Per Mrs. Lyer, Mr. Lyer got upset and decided he would throw away the cell phone (he did not) because it was causing much disruption in their marriage. This man is really a liar.

As these pictures caught her by surprise and then for Mr. Lyer to really lie to her face about it, she did not know what to do, but she felt like causing some serious damage. That "still small voice" inside her however, kept her from making that irrevocable mistake. Do not pretend that you do not know what she is speaking about because you do.

Mr. Lyer's mistress or mistresses, if you are reading this book, you know who you are and what you are, but just in case you are not sure, let me spell it out for you, you are ungodly and unholy women of the world. Sooner or later Mr. Lyer will toss you out like yesterday's trash which is what you have earned. This pains me as I am also married and those women who knowingly sleep with someone else's spouse is exactly what I have said and should be treated as such.

There is more. Mr. Lyer's name is fitting for him as he is the biggest liar. He did not throw away the cell phone; he kept it and continued speaking to his mistress but refused to answer it when Mrs.

Lyer called, as he had previously told her he had thrown it away.

Now this is some **"Cre-Cre"** going on and could cause any woman to snap. I told Mrs. Lyer, I commended her on her strength and courage in the way she handled the situation.

It takes a strong Christian woman to go through what she went through and survived. Mrs. Lyer, you have been through the ringer but you have made it. What Mr. Lyer has done to you is revolting. He is a sex addict and does not care about anyone but his own sexual desires.

Mrs. Lyer confided that she was no longer going to accept that type of behavior and treatment from Mr. Lyer. She was going to take the necessary steps needed to end the faux of a marriage.

My Advice to Mr. & Mrs. Lyer

Mr. Lyer, you are really the worst of the men that I have been told about and written about. Words cannot express my disdain for men like you. You are actually no kind of man and it pains me to know that Mrs. Lyer was even considering staying with you.

You appear to be callous, as you treated Mrs. Lyer like she was nothing to you. After all the years of cheating and the despicable things you did, how can you look at yourself in the mirror?

Maybe that is exactly what you need to do. Take a good look at yourself and see if there is anything of a man or a human being left inside that twisted and sick mind of yours. I am outraged of your disrespect for women on a whole and your mistresses are equally to blame. They do not represent any type of women as they have no class.

Yes, I take this personally as it is very disturbing hearing about the things you did to your beautiful spouse. Divorcing you is not enough, there needs to be a higher punishment. Guess we will have to wait for the man above to render his sentence.

Wait a minute, it is already done. God's word says "Thou shall not commit adultery." It also went on to say, like I previously mentioned, "all adulterers shall have their part in hell". Therefore, you and the mistress or mistresses will be spending an eternity together. You could not get enough of each other, so you will definitely have an eternity together in hell, if you do not repent and confess your sins to God.

Mrs. Lyer, you are one tough lady and I admire you. You are indeed a "Godly" woman, for only such can endure this type of madness and be willing to forgive. Continue to put your trust in God from whence comes all of your help and strength. You have to be smart though, and take care of you and do not let anyone treat you less than how you should be treated.

One last thing, in the event, Mr. Lyer tries to come back, please think twice before giving him the opportunity to hurt you again. Take control of your life and do not be afraid of or intimated by him. He made his decisions but he does not get to choose his consequences.

With him cheating on you, he gave you the right to divorce him as the Bible says "except for the act of adultery, you cannot divorce." Mr. Lyer trampled on your marriage and did not think twice in defiling your bed, so please do not lose any sleep over your decision to divorce him. Celebrate your freedom and move on.

Have no fear, I am sure most, if not all, of my readers are in agreement. You have given him more than what anyone of us would have done. From a human standpoint, I hope that he is as miserable as he made you. However, from a Christian standpoint, I pray that he seeks forgiveness and finds his way back to God.

I do not think anyone is feeling sorry for him and I wonder if any of the mistresses will give him shelter. Maybe he is not so attractive now that he is completely available. They will probably move on to someone else's spouse.

Don't mean to be extra hard on Mr. Lyer, but this was exhausting writing about such horrific situations that he put you through. I am glad you found the strength to do what needed to be done so you can begin to heal, find love, and trust again. He is the lowest of the lows and his misdeeds will eventually catch up with him.

The funny thing about this is Mrs. Lyer was the one with the money. Too bad she did not exercise her power and send him packing. I am sure the reason is when you love you are willing to take chances and give chances.

Mr. Lyer earned the right to be thrown out and Mrs. Lyer confirmed that it was a pleasure tossing him out on the streets, where he belongs with his cell-phone containing the mistress's body parts. Now he could be fulltime with the said mistress/mistresses that he ornately desires.

CHAPTER IX

MR. & MRS. FIREWORKS

Told to me by Mrs. Fireworks – Hispanics

Mr. & Mrs. Fireworks have been married for almost 17 years and have indeed encountered some fireworks throughout this time. They have two children, a boy and a girl; 13 and 16 years of age respectively. Mr. Fireworks is employed at the Fire department as a supervisor and Mrs. Fireworks is employed as a senior director at the Federal Government.

They were high school sweethearts as they dated for most of the duration while they attended and were married immediately after they graduated. There is no one like Mrs. Fireworks and there never will be. She wears the pants in the family and when she tells her "fireman" she is on fire, he definitely makes sure he puts it out, or she will ignite flames that will cause the house to burn down. They basically "light up" the neighborhood with much drama.

I first met Mrs. Fireworks at the beauty shop. She was very vocal and friendly, so we started speaking and we became close friends. This couple can be very loving to each other but Mrs. Fireworks admitted that there has been infidelity on both sides of the spectrum. He did it to her and when she found out, she did it to him.

They broke up for a short period of time, but found their way back to each other. Due to the infidelity, she lost trust in him but is diligently working to regain it and keep the heat on, so that he would have no desire to put out any other personal fires.

Mrs. Fireworks told me that Mr. Fireworks first cheated on her with the neighbor. The neighbor who lives two blocks away is about 12 years their junior so she is young and obviously seeking companionship.

Why does it have to be someone's husband? There are still quite a few single men seeking companionship. Mrs. Fireworks noticed that this particular person spent a considerable amount of time on their block, but she had no idea she was all about her husband. Mrs. Fireworks is not one to play around and she gives it as she takes it. She fights fire with fire.

One night they were about to make love and Mr. Fireworks breakdown and began sobbing. It was at that time, he confessed that he had a one night stand with the neighbor's daughter. Mrs. Fireworks was very upset and distraught. She told me that she felt like "killing her husband and that it was difficult trying to get over his infidelity."

This is something that no one wants to have to deal with. It has to be extremely emotional and heart breaking. When you gave yourself to someone you expect that one to be loyal to you as you are to him and when that does not happen, it takes you to a different place which I am sure is hard to break away from. It would seem that "these guys are not loyal."

Mrs. Fireworks said she had no intention of cheating on him even though he cheated on her but still going through the hurt, pain, sorrow and everything else that goes along with betrayal, she succumbed to the temptation. Ladies, we need to be stronger and not be as weak as these men.

She was driving home one evening and she punctured a tire. In a short period of time, this handsome guy dressed up in army attire drove by and offered to help. She was in awe that he was nice enough to get his hands dirty and changed the tire for a stranger. This reminded her of the good "Samaritan".

Mrs. Fireworks told him she hopes she can repay his kind deed and he invited her for coffee at a coffee shop located in a hotel that was near by. As it turned out he was staying at that said hotel and coffee turned into drinks. Before you know it, she was in his hotel room.

After, it was all over, she felt so ashamed and disgusted that she had now done exactly what he did to her the one thing that she despised, adultery. The next evening at dinner, she confessed to Mr. Fireworks as to what had happened. He was extremely upset, and accused her of being a hypocrite. He moved out the following day and they were separated for approximately three months.

As they have two children together, they attended a baseball game with their 13 year old son. Being in close proximity and the love they share for their son, reminded them of how much they love each other and after the game, Mr. Fireworks took them out to dinner and he decided he belonged with his family.

Have you heard the saying once a cheater always a cheater? Mrs. Fireworks did not see this one coming, but later that same year, they were lying in bed watching TV and the house phone rang. Mr. Fireworks answered and you can tell that he was speaking to a female. Mrs. Fireworks said she got up, reached for the telephone, grabbed it from his hands, and unplugged it from the wall. She was so furious.

Mr. Fireworks had begun a new affair with this lady at work that had attended functions with both him & Mrs. Fireworks. Talk about right under your nose. Well, being caught with his hands in the cookie jar for the second time, Mrs. Fireworks was not having it. She was not going to be in denial and empower him to continue to cheat. No not Mrs. Fireworks.

She gave him the ultimatum, "dump her (the mistress) by telling her in-front of me (Mrs. Fireworks), that the affair is over." If he was not willing to do so, their marriage was over. It was his choice, his spouse or the mistress.

We all know that this would be humbling for any one but especially for a macho firefighter. Will he choose his spouse and children or his mistress? The only way he would be able to do this is if he actually meant it. This was definitely a test of love and we can only hope he passed with "flying colors".

Mrs. Fireworks gave him 24 hours to do what needed to be done or he would have to leave. She told him in no uncertain terms she cannot keep going thorough this and being played like a violin. Those of us who know Mrs. Fireworks knows she is not to be taken for granted. She can fight as dirty as any man.

Mr. Fireworks told Mrs. Fireworks that he needed some time to pull himself together so he can sincerely end the relationship publicly. Imagine you are cheating on your spouse and you are asking for time to break it off. Did you consult with your spouse prior to having an affair? Did she give you permission?

Mrs. Fireworks agreed to give him until the following day and told him they and the mistress will meet and he will let her know then and there, that she (his spouse) is aware of the affair and he has chosen his wife and children over her, (the mistress).

The next day came and they all met at a nearby pub next to the Fire Station. The mistress had no idea why they were meeting but she was about to find out. She thought Mr. Fireworks and her were meeting to hang out, so she was surprised when she saw both of them.

Mr. Fireworks advised the mistress that he was sorry for leading her on and that their relationship is over and not to ever contact him. He further said that as they work together he understands that they will be in each other's company but she is not to speak to him unless it is work related. He went on to say, that his family is his life and he has chosen his family over her.

The mistress became very frantic and emotional and asked how can he do this to their relationship? Could you believe this person? Mrs. Fireworks stopped her in her tracks and asked "you need to ask yourself how you could be with a married man? This is my husband".

Mistress, you know that he is married; you also personally know his wife and you still engaged in this affair? You had no concern for his family, you just knew that you wanted him and did not consider the fact that he has a family. Mrs. Fireworks said to her, how you dare have an attitude, you have no rights to my husband.

Again I ask, mistress, what were you hoping for? Don't you know when a man is faced with his family over someone "easy" like you, 99% of the time, he chooses his family. Mrs. Fireworks went on to tell her, "have some pride and class and stay away from married men, especially my spouse, he is not available to you or anyone else."

Mrs. Fireworks continued "find yourself someone who is into you alone, and look away even if you are attracted to him because in the end, all you end up with is a broken heart." Single women, There are single men looking for love, just be patient. Playing with Mr. Fireworks or anyone else's spouse is not the answer. Think about having a spouse and another person wanting him/her, how would you feel?

When I caught up with Mrs. Fireworks she told me that life was good and they were rebuilding the trust they had for each other. She believes this time around he was going to be true to their marriage. She also told me that they were also considering counseling to help solidify their relationship. In addition, she mentioned that there was a significant difference in both of their lives and the way they express their love to each other. Even the children, were the happiest they had ever been.

My Advice to Mr. & Mrs. Fireworks

You both have a long road ahead but you are committed to making your marriage work and keeping each other happy. Please do not be distracted with the temptation that is around you. Stay focus on your family and be happy.

Will you be tempted? Yes you will but remember to look to God from whence cometh your help. Stay in his word and stay connected to each other by having family, prayer and quality time together. Remember how it was when you first met and how much you have loved each other over the years.

When you are feeling disconnected from each other, look inside yourself, or just look at your children and you will know this is something you have put together and it is worth fighting for. Don't be quick to give up and please continue to seek counseling. Know that I am here for you and you can reach me at any time.

CHAPTER X

MR. & MRS. WRIGHT

Told to me by Mrs. Wright & from my observation - West Indians

Mr. & Mrs. Wright are exactly like their name, they are just right. In the midst of all the madness we have read about the other couples, there is true love and admiration actually taking place with this couple. Married for 25 years, Mr. & Mrs. Wright were blessed with a son age 22 married with no children and an adopted son Age 21 focusing on his career.

Could you imagine being married for twenty five years and never one day had to worry about your spouse being unfaithful, this is exactly what is happening here with this lovely couple, who are dear to me. Mrs. Wright and I basically grew up together. We went to the same schools. I am older, but of course, I do look younger. Mr. Wright is about seven years older than Mrs. Wright. The happy couple met when Mrs. Wright was just about 16 years, but thought she was grown. She is about 4' 9" tall and Mr. Wright about 5' 6". What did I tell you, they are just right in more ways than "one".

Prior to Mrs. Wright being married, because she was under age, when she met Mr. Wright, dating was not allowed. Her dad was very strict and nothing bypassed him, especially when it came to his children. Mr. Wright, however did not give up and continued to maintain contact with the now Mrs. Wright.

As time went by, Mrs. Wright graduated from high school at the age of seventeen and when she turned 18, Mr. Wright asked her dad permission to date. Keep in mind he is five years older, so her dad does not want to hear it. He basically dismissed Mr. Wright. To Mrs. Wright's dad, "why you have to be so rude, don't you know Mr. Wright is human too?" (We all understood when we became parents).

Mr. Wright was not a citizen, so that was an additional hill he had to climb with her dad. They saw each other occasionally and Mr. Wright was very persistent. He found the girl of his dreams and he was not giving up.

He continued to pursue her and they decided to date even though her dad was not sold on Mr. Wright. Time went by and they got engaged. Shortly thereafter, they were married. I was out of the country and was unable to attend, but I saw the video and the pictures. I must say it was a beautiful wedding and the fact that they are extremely happy, is a blessing. This is what happens when you find your soul mate.

Her dad, though he was a little extreme in protecting his daughters, by this time, he had somewhat softened for her sake but still kept a close eye on Mr. Wright, just in case he turned into Mr. Wrong.

The Wrights were blessed with a bouncing baby boy two years later and they could not be happier. This child was as energetic as his dad. If you saw them together, they all looked like siblings instead of parents and child. Basically, they were all close in height. This child was allowed to travel by himself from the time he was seven years old. He thought he was grown.

A year later, this couple adopted a son, as they found out that they could not have any more children. They wanted a brother for their son and lucky for them they were able to adopt a one-month old baby boy.

Mr. & Mrs. Wright do everything together. When I say everything, I mean just that, everything. They work, shop, have lunch, travel, exercise and play together. Wherever you see one, you see the other. They are never alone.

Mr. Wright is a flirt but a harmless one. Everyone loves him and he is adorable. As a matter of fact, so is Mrs. Wright but she is sometimes a "pain". She is very shy due to her sheltered upbringing and it is hard for her to be forthright and get her talking, but once that happens, there is no end to the madness.

Mrs. Wright and one of her sisters are extremely close. They curse each other but they love each other. I often refer to them as CNN. On a serious note, you can call on the Wrights to assist you with anything you need; especially Mr. Wright and he will do it for you but will first consult with Mrs. Wright.

As previously stated, the Wrights do not do any thing without first consulting with each other. This is how a real couple should be, without secrets. Their lives to each other are an open book. They know where each other is at all times and are in constant communication.

How many of you wish this was your life? Others may say it is boring. Maybe it can be, but for this couple, when I see them, I do not see boredom. I see a very happy couple enjoying quality time with each other and making others around them feel welcome. I see a couple that means every word they said on their wedding day.

They are a great example to married couples throughout the nation. Not only are they kind to each other, they are kind to their family and friends. Just to share an example with you of their kindness. There are of course many more that I can share, but this one stands out.

Mr. & Mrs. Wonderful were spending Christmas out of town and around the same time my children and I were in town visiting with my relatives. The Wrights allowed us to stay at their brand new home for the duration, no questions asked.

The only issue I have with the Wrights is they can be just a little paranoid sometimes with their electrical equipments. They will repetitiously tell you what to do or not do with their sophisticated appliances. Since they are very dear to the family, we spend as much time together as time would allow and we converse daily.

Mr. Wright once said to me. "I do not understand how anyone can cheat. It is nasty." He also stated that if he cheated on his wife, he cannot be with her again. In addition, he said that he has had opportunities to do just that, but he took the high road and went on to say "It is not appealing to me, as I have everything I need in my spouse."

Mr. Wright is really what epitomizes a loving and faithful spouse. He showers Mrs. Wright with compliments and praises. When you see them together they always have a smile on their faces. This indicates happiness. I have never seen them argue angrily and if they disagree, it is not with negativity or disrespect, it is tastefully done.

Everyone wants a Mr. Wright, so how lucky is Mrs. Wright? Extremely lucky! She hung in there, despite her father's disapproval and she has just the right partner. I am sure her dad is smiling now. Mrs. Wright and Mr. Wright are the real deal of what true love is all about and it seems like this marriage was indeed made in heaven.

My Advice to Mr. & Mrs. Wright

Mr. & Mrs. Wright, you are two of a kind. Keep doing what you are doing to each other and for each other. Do not listen to those who say they cannot be with their spouse 24-7. Deep down, they wish they could. Continue to love on each other and shower each other with everything that you have inside and out.

You are an inspiration to most and it is refreshing to know there are couples like you in the world. You seem to be like our current President and First Lady. Be a testimony for those who are married and are discouraged and a light for those who inspire to be married but are afraid because of the many broken marriages.

Spread the love of Christ and the love you have found in each other, so that all may see and know that God's word does not return unto him void, "for he who finds a wife finds a good thing". Let others know that marriage does not have to be painful and miserable. That is not what God intended it to be. Therefore, as married couples we need to re-examine the way we interact with our partners. Marriage is supposed to be two people loving and enjoying each other in the good and the bad, the ups and the downs. As the song writer sings, "God gave me you for the ups and downs!"

You have exemplified what marriage is about and you are to be commended for your faithfulness to each other as you have lived up to what each one should contribute in a marriage, 100%.

My encouragement to you, my friends, is to continue to do what you are doing and do not let anyone or anything negatively influence you. Remain truthful to each other and continue to be each other's best friend.

One more thing, do not get high-minded and take each other for granted. No one is above reproach when it comes to the Devil. His job is to dismantle families and relationships, especially the ones that seem to be on solid ground.

I admire both of you and know that God will continue to bless, strengthen and keep you, as you seek to do his will. You are indeed a blessing to all and I pray that you will be faithful in your commitment to Christ and your marriage, that others may be inspired to do the same.

CHAPTER XI

MR. & MS. FANTASY

An Emotional Affair – Told to me by Mr. & Ms. Fantasy (European/Bahamian)

For Mr. & Ms. Fantasy it was friendship at first sight. Ever since they met about 20 years ago, they have been emotionally involved. During this time they have both been married to different people. However, it happens that when one of them is married the other is not and vice versa.

Mr. & Ms. Fantasy are not a couple. They are simply two people that are fond of each other and as a result have been involved emotionally for almost two decades. Currently Mr. Fantasy is married and Ms. Fantasy is not. This couple is very unique. Basically, from my conversation with Ms. Fantasy, they continue to do everything together except physical sexual activity.

Ms. Fantasy told me that they met at a time when both of them were going through marital problems. They care deeply for each other and they know what each other is thinking before it is spoken. In addition, she said, they can be in a crowded room and they only have eyes for each other.

Ms. Fantasy and I are close and she introduced me to Mr. Fantasy, who I would say is a "heart throb". I can definitely see why Ms. Fantasy is attracted to him, as he demonstrates a warm and sincere quality. Mr. Fantasy also told me that he is very fond of Ms. Fantasy and she will always have a special place in his heart.

I almost cried. Here are two people that apparently love each other, more than most married couples do, but they know they cannot be together in the "Biblical" sense. Ms. Fantasy told me this in one of our conversations.

In addition, Ms. Fantasy advised that it was easy for her to be drawn into Mr. Fantasy's, fantasy as he is the most caring, loving and funniest person she has ever met. (Not to overlook his physical attributes), she said.

Over the years, Ms. Fantasy said there were times that they became very close and were tempted to take their relationship further but she could not do it, as she is a good girl. Ms. Fantasy admitted to me that she sometimes dreams about him and envisions what it would be like to be with him, but then she pinches herself for thinking that way. Pinch yourself very hard Ms. Fantasy, he is married. Please do not cross the line. You are my friend, but I have to be true to my beliefs.

Surprisingly, Mr. Fantasy also told me that he had several dreams about him and Ms. Fantasy and that just goes to show that they both are thinking of each other, whether that is healthy or not, you be the judge!

What fascinates me about them is they light up when they are speaking to and about each other. I am not sure they realize it, but their faces and voices reflect how deeply they care about each other. You will have to be blind not to see it.

In addition, Ms. Fantasy said that Mr. Fantasy calls her every day, multiple times a day regardless of where he is, in/out of the country and tells her he misses her. Oh!! My heart is touched, for sometimes, not even spouses call to say, I miss you.

No wonder she is having an emotional affair with Mr. Fantasy. Truth be told, most of us probably would if we were in that situation. Yes I said it. Again, Christian or non-Christian, we are humans and everyone likes when someone is attentive to them.

Ms. Fantasy further advised that one of the times she was really touched was a valentine's day. He was getting ready to go out with his now former spouse, and he took the time to call her and wished her Happy Valentines' Day.

She said this was one of the times when he was going through his divorce but the gentleman that he is, still was willing to take his now former spouse to lunch. This is very interesting.

She went on to say, that as a woman, you are going to feel special, as you did not expect this, and this handsome man took the time to call you and say Happy Valentine's Day. Makes me feel like this is someone we would all like to know.

I know some of you are saying if Mr. Fantasy is so great and caring, why did he divorce? I asked Ms. Fantasy this question and her response was, "not because you are nice, that does not mean the other person is." Ladies this is true. Please know I am not defending Mr. Fantasy, but let us not be quick to render judgment in this case, as we do not know the facts.

The one thing Mr. Fantasy shared with me is that the former spouse had low self-esteem and complained about everything. In addition, he said that she totally "let herself go." I imagine he meant she stopped taking care of herself. Ladies, whatever you did to get him, you have to do to keep him. Do not become complacent, as your spouse did not lose his eyesight when he said "I do".

He further mentioned that Ms. Fantasy on the other hand makes him laugh and he finds her adorable. He knows he is married but said "it is what it is." I told him that I can see how much he and Ms. Fantasy admire each other but I told him he does belong to someone else, so they cannot cross the line.

Further more, I reminded him that Ms. Fantasy is one of my best friends and we sometimes talk for hours and hours. Therefore, if anything is going on, I know she will tell me. She is such a joy to be around and she makes all her friends feel that they matter. I do not want to see her hurt by him or anyone else. Her last relationship ended badly so I want the best for her next time around.

He did say that he adores Ms. Fantasy so much, he finds himself talking about her even when he does not plan to. I said to him "Mr. Fantasy, you have it bad for Ms. Fantasy." I further told him if he continues to speak about Ms. Fantasy to his spouse, sooner or later, she is going to ask herself, why he speaks continuously speaks of her. I do not think he can help himself. When you are into someone, you cannot help but speak about that person every chance you get. I suddenly realized that Mr. Fantasy is in love with Ms. Fantasy but he cannot admit it since he is a married man. I am sure Ms. Fantasy is also in love with him.

Ms. Fantasy told me that when they first met, she believes it was instant chemistry and it has only grown over the years. She went on to say that they both try to deny it at times, but in their hearts they know what they feel and know it is there to stay.

This sounds like the story of two hearts that want to be together, but because of who they are they cannot. They are doing the right thing. If only more people were like this, there would be less broken marriages.

I like both Mr. & Ms. Fantasy and if you meet them, you would too. It is so much fun being in their presence. They actually act like two little kids at times. How amazing that some people can bring out the best in you or should I say the "kid" in you. That is a good thing. Better to have someone bring out the best than the worse. However, I pray that you do not cross that line!

Anyone who has come in contact with them can immediately see the chemistry and the caring they have for each other. Neither of the two will admit it but it is indisputable and only time will tell, if they will ever get together in the Biblical sense. Funny, I should say Biblical sense, considering what I have to write next. Seems like I am being pulled into this fantasy, "time out", please!

Ms. Fantasy had me laughing for quite sometime one day. I laughed so loud and so long, I thought I was not going to be able to stop. She said to me, that at one time they talked about getting together and she told him that he would have to wait seven years and when the seven years were up she told him, he would have to wait another seven years.

What a patient man, it is almost 21 years. Will that be the day that they let their guards down and go for the gusto? Ms. Fantasy further advised me that I might say that they are getting old, but she reminded me that age is only a number, besides, she only gets better with age and they are both in their early 40's.

If you are thinking that the two "seven - years" wait were hilarious Ms. Fantasy told me she had a better one for me. Readers, I hope you are ready for this one. She said to me, "I want you to sit for this one" and she proceeded to tell me that Mr. Fantasy, with his fine self told her that he is not 100% European, he is 50% black.

She said it caught her by surprise, so she asked him about his family tree to which he said "it is not about my family tree it is about me as a person." She said she was even more confused so she said "I am not sure I understand what you mean."

Mr. Fantasy, said to her very quietly, "listen, I may be "white on top, but I am totally black from the waist down." I could not believe what I was hearing. I was in shock and speechless for sometime, then, I started laughing and laughed for quite some time. After I stopped, all I could say was, he did not say that, this is too much!

She said "I kid you not" and also said what was so funny is that he actually believed it and felt very proud that he was black from the waist down. I had no further comment and to this day, Ms. Fantasy, often reminds me of when she told me that and said I should have seen the look on my face, she said it was priceless. As I said, I cannot speak to this and I am therefore, leaving this for the readers to digest.

Mr. Fantasy you have it real bad for Ms. Fantasy and would like her to think about you in that way. Have you forgotten you are married? I have been in both of their company so I know a little or more than I should know about Mr. Fantasy as well.

Mr. Fantasy told me that at one time Ms. Fantasy told him she was never going to speak with him. He said he was so distraught of the idea, as he cannot imagine life without her. He further said it was at that time, he in no uncertain terms, told Ms. Fantasy how much she meant to him and how much he wanted to be with her. This reminds me of when I first fell in love. Lucky for me, my Mr. Fantasy (my husband) was single and disengaged.

Ms. Fantasy said when they are together they are like two little kids on the play ground. Fighting each other and cannot get enough of each other. If you ask me, I think the reason they fight is the way they express themselves so they could be close to each other. She further said he is very endearing to her and does not have a problem displaying affection, even if it is just a touch on her cheeks or his favorite spot, her chin.

Her words to me were that she enjoys every moment of his touch. She does pranks on him all the time from ice in his shirt to marks on his hands when she could get the crayons away from him. These are like two little kids enjoying what time they can have with each other. I am touched but at the same time worried for these two. They are too much into each other and I am afraid the inevitable will eventually happen.

Mr. Fantasy also told me that he enjoys Ms. Fantasy's company and he adores her. Any time she is upset with him, he does what is necessary to make her feel better and shows her how much he cares. He also had me laughing as he said that sometimes it could be as much as fifty close hugs in the space of two minutes. What can I say? Ms. Fantasy is his fantasy. I also internalized, and asked "who is this guy? What a guy!" Ladies, stop fantasizing.

Mr. Fantasy also shared with me that when he dreams about Ms. Fantasy, he is sad when he realizes it is only a dream. He also mentioned that he speaks of her often not only to his spouse but to his close friends.

In my opinion the reason why he speaks about her is because she is always in his thoughts and he enjoys talking about her. This means he does have special feelings for her and I am sure she does for him. It is obvious that they feed off each other.

He went on to tell me that sometimes wherever he goes, he sees different people and they remind him of her. It seems like Mr. Fantasy really fantasies about Ms. Fantasy. Mr. Fantasy further mentioned that he teases her so many times and he enjoys seeing the various reactions from her.

Married couples, I am not condoning this fantasy, but you need to adapt some things from Mr. & Ms. Fantasy. The main take away is for you to be playful with your spouse, it goes a long way and it keeps you youthful. I think the reason why they have so much fun together is because they are really good friends and really love each other. Again, I am not condoning this emotional affair. However, it is refreshing to see that although these two people are not really a couple, they seem to really care for each other.

Another take away, married couples, is to keep the communication line open. If you hurt your spouse's feelings, do something about it and make him/her feel better. Don't let time go by for it to fester and you walk around being mad. Most of all become each other's best friend, and it will be easy to be friendly to each other at all times.

If you like each other it is easy to love one another and not be quick to be upset. Mr. & Ms. Fantasy seem like a fantasy but they are real people with real feelings and we can learn from them.

I have to ask a few questions to us married folks.

How many of us daydream of being with someone other than our spouse?

How many of us desire to be with someone if only for one minute, one night, one week, one month, or one year?

How many of us, wish our spouse treated us like Mr. & Ms. Fantasy treat each other?

How many of us yearn for the playfulness, the simple touch on our face or chin that these two express to each other?

How many of us would have an emotional affair if we find the right person?

How many of us have had an emotional affair?

How many of us are currently engaging in an emotional affair?

How many of us engaging in an emotional affair, do not want to give it up as it gives us something we are not receiving from home?

How many of us are enjoying the emotional affair and does not see anything wrong?

How many of us wish we could find that special someone that fills in where our spouse does not?

What is an emotional affair?

An emotional affair is cheating emotionally with someone.

It is confiding in someone besides your spouse.

It is finding pleasure in someone else's company than we do with our spouse or significant other.

It is dreaming about that John Doe or Mary Jane and wishing you could be with that person.

It is basically being in a sexless relationship.

It is an emotional game and warfare.

I would imagine it is exhilarating and riveting.

It is my belief that at least 75% of the population are guilty of this type of affair and it is said that it is a refuge for women who do not want to physically cheat on their spouses but do not mind confiding in the opposite sex and seeing them as a "best" friend.

Ladies, we have a lot of thinking and examining to do. "Who cheats more than a Politician"? Food for thought as we enjoy our fantasies or awaken from our nightmares!

My Advice to Mr. & Ms. Fantasy

Mr. Fantasy, life is short and if you were not married I would say enjoy Ms. Fantasy and take comfort in knowing that although you cannot be together physically, you are in each others hearts and it looks like you will always be.

You are, however, married. Therefore, the following is the only advice I can give to you.

Mr. Fantasy, enjoy your spouse or divorce her and marry your fantasy.

You are not being fair to your spouse or to Ms. Fantasy.

What exactly are you getting from Ms. Fantasy that you are not getting from your spouse?

What if your spouse finds out about your true fantasy?

Why do you find so much time to think about Ms. Fantasy?

If you are always thinking about Ms. Fantasy when do you think about your spouse?

Do you think it is fair to have Ms. Fantasy holding on to the fantasy of being together, when you have a spouse?

Ms. Fantasy, I can only imagine what you are going through. I understand that you are single and you have strong feelings for Mr. Fantasy the same way he does for you, but he is married, so there is a conflict. You need to ask yourself the following?

Will he ever be free to be with you?

Why can't you be free simultaneously so you can take the opportunity to explore your feelings?

If he divorces his spouse how do you know you will still be his fantasy, or will he find another?

I know how much you both care and love each other, so I will say this, if in the event, life throws you the opportunity where you are both available, follow your hearts and your feelings and see where this fantasy takes you.

To both of you, it is only then you will know for sure if you were meant to be. It is only then you can follow your hearts and throw caution to the wind.

At this time you cannot, you cannot cross that line. So not to be funny, but "if you cannot be with the one you love, please love the one you are with" and set aside this fantasy.

Seek God's guidance and wisdom to make the right decision, whatever it may turn out to be.

CHAPTER XII

MR. & MRS. TODMAN

My Personal Story

I would be remiss to speak about eight couples and not speak about my marriage. My spouse and I have been married for 34 years and have been blessed with three lovely children; two boys and a girl. Our children are grown and two of them are on their own, one of them being married. Our last child recently graduated from college and is temporarily back at home.

Throughout our marriage, there have been many challenges. The burning question I know you readers have is whether or not any of us cheated. Personally, I do not believe in cheating, so no, I have not cheated on my spouse, at least not physically. The other question is if Mr. T. cheated.

As I previously stated, we have been married for 34 years. In marriage, that is considered several lifetimes. So ask yourself the question in 34 years, have you been married at least six years and of those six years, did your spouse cheat on you?

Those of you who know me know I tend to be a little naïve and gullible, but one thing I am not is foolish. Every one would like to know and believe that they are the person that has the faithful spouse but that is not always the case. David was a man after God's own heart and he cheated. This however does not give anyone a pass to cheat.

Am I saying my spouse cheated and am I condoning cheating? No, I am not. Let us ask Mr. T. Mr. T., the readers would like to know, have you ever cheated on Mrs. T. and if you have, how many times, and are you still cheating? I believe that is an answer that only God, Mr. T., the woman or women involved and maybe the spouse, (that would be me) know. Yes, I may have my opinion and may have suspicions like any other spouse but am I going to throw my children's "daddy" under the bus? No. In writing this book, I thought about approaching it from various angles and this is the one I decided on.

Therefore, for the sake of my family, especially my children, I will say that our marriage has had all types of twists, turns, and many, yes many disputes. We have been married for more than half of each other's lives.

The important thing is that we recently celebrated our 34th wedding anniversary and we do believe that "what God has joined together, let no one put asunder." Now, the "haters" can ask, "what if God did not put you together?" I will say to you the issue with marriages is not that God did anything wrong, but humans fall short of doing what is right.

Just to reiterate, we are married and we do not plan on divorcing any time soon. At least that is the way we feel at this moment. Therefore, the women or men that maybe waiting in the wings, you might as well give up as it is going to be a long wait. In the interim, however, I will try to answer the fiery questions that some of you may have.

Q&A

Am I a saint? No. I am not and Mr. T. is really far from one.

Do we like each other at all times? No we do not.

Do we hate each other ways, at times? Yes we do.

Have we been disrespectful at times to each other? Yes we have.

Have we yelled and called each other names? Yes.

Have we said horrible things to each other? Yes.

Have we asked ourselves the question why did we get married? Yes we have.

Have there been times we cursed each other? Yes.

Have we been accusatory towards one another? Yes we have.

Have we slept in separate beds in our home? Yes we have.

Have we gone to bed mad? Yes.

Have we been at home and not spoken to each other? Yes

Have we ever pretended to get along? Yes.

Have we attended events while mad at each other? Yes we have.

We can go on and on about what we have, or have not done, or felt, but let us look at a more positive perspective.

Do we trust each other? Yes, but he trusts me more.

Do we love each other? Yes we do.

Do we care deeply for each other? Yes, very much.

Do we plan on divorcing? As of now, No we do not.

Do we spend quality time together? Yes, as often as we can.

Do we make each other laugh? Sometimes

Are we passionate for each other? Yes we are.

Do we enjoy each other's company? Most of the time, we do.

Do we want to stay married? Most of the time, we do.

Do we forgive each other when necessary? Sometimes we do.

Do we have sex or make love? Both

Do we imagine what it would be like to have been with another person? Yes, but don't most of you?

Would we like to be married to other people? Absolutely not, and that is how we feel today.

Do we love each other? Yes passionately.

Are we protective of each other? Yes, we are. Mr. T. is more protective of me.

Life's Journey

Just in case you are not satisfied with the Q&A, let me take you on a romantic journey throughout our lives, so you could understand how we got here and that we are here to stay as a married couple. We are married for Life.

I grew up in a family of ten. Six girls and two boys with two parents and consider myself to be the most outgoing and definitely the most outspoken of my siblings. What you see is what you get. I am also a loving person and always willing to help and I love to laugh.

Some have said my laugh is infectious and my smile is captivating. Yes, that is what I have been told. In addition, my name is very unique so let me just say, "thank you Mom, I love you." Regarding Mr. T., he also grew up in a family of ten, three boys, five girls and two parents.

Although I have three children and the last one recently graduated, I have been told that I do not look a day over "39". That is correct. I have also been told that I am full of myself and I do not need a cheerleading squad. I am very self-confident, which is one of the attractive and appealing qualities about me.

I feel I do exude confidence in a classy manner. Maybe I am in love with myself. Well, I think I am and that is a good thing. In order to love others, you ought to first love yourself. If you do not love yourself, chances are you will also have difficulty accepting love.

So where did I grow up? I grew up in the British Virgin Islands and had a front view to the beach and everything in the bay area. Imagine living five minutes away from the beach but being afraid of the water. To this day, my siblings and I cannot swim.

Looking back we were poor, even though we did not know it because there was always something for lunch and dinner, even if dinner was a repeat of lunch. We were happy and looked out for each other. My dad worked in St. Thomas, U.S.V.I. and was gone most of the time, so my mom was the head of the household in that respect, as she was always around.

At the age of nine, I gave my heart to Christ and have been a Christian ever since. Each day, I experience new mercies from Him and will not change being a child of God for five minutes of worldly pleasures. Many have told me that I need to take some time and explore what I did not do in my teenage years. I say it is unnecessary. I am very happy with life.

My older sisters were part of a Bible youth group but I was not old enough to attend, therefore, I slipped out and went with them each time. So I presume you can say I was a little rebel, but in a good way.

The first time I met my spouse was during a primary school spelling B competition. No it was not love at first sight, even though, he was very bright, handsome, and had a deep voice. He was the lead competitor, but my school was not intimidated by him. We won some and lost some. To hear Mr. T. tell it, I am sure he would say his school won it all. That was not the case.

At the age of 12, I attended high school and was very afraid of boys. Yes, very much so. I thought if I spoke to them, I would become pregnant. Therefore, no matter how "fine" they were, and most of them were really "fine", I ran away and kept my distance for fear of becoming pregnant.

My mom did not tell me about the birds and the bees, so it was up to me to figure it all out. Thankfully, I had older sisters, so I watched and learned about growing up and becoming a woman. It was very interesting as I observed what was going on with my older sisters.

High school was a great time for me as I was becoming a young woman and saw my body changing before my eyes. Of course, I was "cute," and with so much hair on my head, I experimented with various hair styles and constantly received positive feedback. I was known as "the cute girl with a lot of hair." That is one of the things, Mr. T. misses, my lovely hair.

I tied for "first place" with another student as the winner of the afro competition during my senior year. Unfortunately, I do not have a picture to share but it was absolutely beautiful. Use your imagination and go back in time (ok, not too far).

Mr. T. also attended high school but we were not in the same class. He walked around campus as if he was "God's gift to women" and as though he could have any girl he wanted. Therefore, I totally ignored him and did not even say "hi". I knew he was trying to get my attention but remember I was afraid of guys. However, even if I was not, I would not have been interested, as he was very "cocky" with his "fine" self.

Later on, in High School, I dated, nothing serious, just held hands. I remember this one guy that was about four years older than me and was already out of high school, also attended my church. He was very tall, extremely handsome and played the bass guitar. Yes, something about the "bass".

My sisters and I attended a Saturday night concert in which the bass guitar player participated. When the concert ended, he escorted us home and he and I stayed outside for a little bit and talked. Not even a kiss took place, but when I went inside, brushed my teeth and went to bed, my mom whipped me.

She whipped me for staying outside, on the front patio and speaking to a guy. Mom, I love you, but what was that all about? I am surprised that none of us became a "Nun" considering how strict we were brought up. Nothing against Nuns, it has to be your calling and we were not called.

As we were primarily a family of girls, my parents were very strict, so we grew up in a bubble. To this day, as previously mentioned I am the bravest and most outspoken of my siblings, both sisters and brothers. I tell it like it is and encourage others to do the same. Mr. T. is even more outspoken but sometimes in an arrogant way. He can also be very charming but is a tiger at times. Yes, he is. Despite all his imperfections, I love him dearly and I know he loves me.

The Pursuit

Having graduated from High School (age 17), I rarely saw Mr. T. and the few times I saw him, there he was with one earring in his left ear, driving a red sports car with black stripes and "eyeing" me, as though I had something he wanted.

One day, while I was waiting on my transportation to take me home, Mr. T. drove by and asked if I needed a ride home and I told him "no" and looked away. The next time I saw him, it was outside my place of employment and again, he asked if I needed a ride home, to which I again, said, no.

Why did he keep bothering me? Now one night, I attended my church to view the film "The Burning Hell" and there he showed up right next to me and asked "is this seat taken? I said "no". He further asked "do you mind if I sit next to you, I said "no." It seems like I basically had one word for Mr. T., and it was "no".

During intermission, Mr. T. turned to me and asked "what are you doing on Saturday night?" I asked "why?" He said, "I would like to take you out to dinner." I replied, "I will have to check my calendar." Keep in mind I am now about 18, what calendar do I have and need to check at that age?

He said to me "ok, can you let me know on Friday?" I said "sure," all the while knowing that I had no intention of going out with him. I just did not like him.

Friday night came and again, he sat by me in Youth Fellowship at the Church. I tried not to look at him basically I tried not to even breathe. I knew he was waiting for the opportunity to find out, if I was going to go out with him and I had no interest, so I just wanted to ignore him and hopefully, he will go away.

After church, I immediately went into the church's bus to avoid him seeing or questioning me. It felt good that I dodged that bullet. I just did not want to be bothered by this guy and he was continuously hot on my trail.

The Saturday, however, my best friend at the time, and I were walking along the bay and there we saw him and his cousin walking toward us. I brought my friend up to speed about how he was trying to get with me and that I had ignored him.

His cousin, whom he was with, was interested in my best friend and we joked about it and asked "why are they in our space, why don't they stay in their own community?" They lived about twenty minutes away.

When they got close to where we were standing, Mr. T. walked towards me, grabbed my hand, and politely asked "can I speak to you for a minute?" I pulled away from him and said "what do you want?" He asked "weren't you suppose to give me an answer, if you are going to go out with me tonight?"

I thought to myself, this guy needs to go away and leave me alone. He needs to get a life. I responded and said to him, "yes I was to give you an answer and the answer is no." After that, I walked back to my girlfriend and we laughed hysterically and disappeared from their presence.

Did I notice that he was hurt? Yes I did, but it did not bother me. My goal was to make it difficult for him. That is the only way I would have known if he was serious. If he could endure the insults and rejections, then I would know if it was worth giving him a chance.

As time went by, he began coming to my church regularly. He became a member and attended the youth group. He continued to pursue me to no avail. So how much longer, before I would agree to go out with him?

The Connection

It all happened one night when he volunteered to take the lead in a major vocal part to be performed during a youth group conference. The person selected to lead the most important song, was not up to par, so he took the mike and began singing and all the girls went crazy over his voice. It was electrifying.

From there, all the girls in the youth group were interested and I decided I was not about to let him become interested in anyone else, so I knew I had to minimize playing "hard to get". Some of the girls even started playing with his nice soft hair. Yes, there was a nice bunch on his head but he lost some and he decided to shave away what was left. He said he was not going to walk around with a "donut hole" in his head. That was not cool, and he supposedly was this "macho" guy.

He continued to pursue me and still did not make any headway. He would send messages to me through mutual friends, leave me telephone messages and I still would not budge. I knew at some point I will break but I was determined to make him sweat for as long as possible.

During this time, the youth conference was in progress. The night of the concert, I spotted him walking along the bay with a mutual friend and of course I felt a little jealous but still did not speak with him.

The youth conference was swiftly coming to an end and was closing out with a banquet. They needed volunteers to do various things to bring it together and make it a great evening. I volunteered to help and I did not have a car but could easily have asked my brother in law to pick me up. However, I had a different car in mind.

I contacted Mr. T. and asked if he could give me a ride (a car ride). He was enthused and said yes. It made me feel good. He was on cloud nine. To him, he finally made a connection and felt that there was hope.

I always loved fashion and have always been a sassy dresser and have been told I was and still am extremely attractive. For the banquet, I purchased this beautiful soft blue long, clinging hi-low dress. It was absolutely gorgeous and I bought it with Mr. T. in mind. I sure did.

I meant I was going to "dress to kill". The evening of the event came and everyone was riding on the Church's bus that evening. I was picked up first and when we got to Mr. T's house, he was also "dressed to kill".

The Confession

Six feet tall, 175 lbs and in a lovely custom made blue suit, almost the same color as the dress I was wearing, stood this fine young man. This was so surreal. He got on the bus and sat right next to me. Yes.

The heat that was in the bus was almost enough to make you sing Nelly song, "It's getting hot in here". Oops! It was not around then. Everyone on the bus felt the magic in the air and knew something was going to happen that night.

I could not deny the undeniable and admitted to him that I was ready to go out with him and be his girlfriend. We spoke all through the night at the dinner and had our first kiss that evening. It was magical and we have not stopped kissing since.

We started dating and the heat continued to sizzle. This guy was hot, was loving, handsome, thoughtful and had everything a girl wanted and needed. When he touched me and held me, I melted in his arms and did not want to be let go. I knew this was the one for me from that first kiss. I said to myself, I have found my husband.

We made our own music and we listened to music as we held each other close and danced the nights away. It was me and my honey against all odds. We were totally committed to each other and did not have eyes for anyone else. We had found our soul mate in each other. What a beautiful courtship it was.

Mr. T. and I spent so much time on the beach, in the theatre, visiting each other's family and just hanging out. One year into dating, he relocated to St. Thomas and prior to leaving, we became engaged.

We missed each other so much that each weekend, we will alternate the visits between St. Thomas and Tortola. We had to see each other and spend quality time together. We had so much fun doing things together and taking the time to know and understand each other.

One year following our engagement, we were married. It was a very intimate ceremony with very close family and friends. We spent our honeymoon in Puerto Rico (lots of honey in the moon). Following, the honeymoon I relocated and joined my new husband in St. Thomas. It took some adjusting though, as I missed my family and was homesick.

I wondered if I had made the right decision to be married and leave my family behind. I realized at that time, that I did not know anything about this man and I was miles away from my family.

During the first year, we sometimes argued, slammed doors and were mad with each other at times. This was all part of growing up and understanding it is not easy living with someone. We soon learned that marriage is not as easy as it seems.

It takes a lot of hard work. At one time I became so mad, I packed a suitcase and said I was leaving and not coming back. I was overwhelmed, did not feel that I was receiving the attention needed from him and wanted to leave forever.

However, when I got outside, I heard footsteps coming down the stairs. I became scared and went back inside. Lucky for me, Mr. T. did not lock the door, so I was able to get back inside.

The person coming down the stairs was a mutual friend coming unannounced to visit. At times I wonder what would have happened had I not heard those footsteps. What would have happened if I had left two minutes earlier?

Would I have indeed left my husband or would I have stayed. No one knows. I do feel however, what happened was meant to be. Our friend was meant to be there at that particular time walking down those stairs to scare me back into the house.

Maybe I was being protected from what would have been out there in the world that night waiting to cause harm. I do not know and I would never know. One thing I do know, God always protects his children. I have no regrets in staying and as a result, I was blessed beyond measure with a beautiful family that I will not trade for the world. My experiences have made me who I am, and I am happy with me.

Family Expansion/Relocation

I became pregnant the following year and we gave birth to a beautiful baby boy. He was a joy and looked just like his dad. It was hard for me to place him with a baby sitter but we found a lovely lady who took care of him and I enrolled in college part time.

After approximately one and a half years I completed my Associates degree in Executive Administration and worked at the University of the Virgin Islands. I loved the Virgin Islands and my job but I felt it was time for a change.

We wanted more for our family and knew it was time to explore the universe. After several considerations and brainstorming, we decided to move to Florida. My husband came about two weeks prior to me. He bought a house, a car and was all set for my arrival. I loved our new home and was excited about the new life we were starting in Florida.

By this time, our first born, was approximately five years old and was very intelligent. He was always making A's and way ahead of the other children. To this day, he continues to excel. Six years after, we gave birth to an amazingly beautiful baby girl and four years later unexpectedly, gave birth to another handsome baby boy.

Therefore, during the first thirteen years of marriage, we gave birth to three beautiful children, who mean everything to us. Even though they are grown, they are the ones that keep us going. They bring us great joy!

All three of them are artistically gifted and are currently working on their careers. They do have the potential to become very successful. In addition to artistically talented, they are academically geniuses as well. Two of them graduated with perfect GPA's and the other with an above average GPA from their respective universities.

We are proud of our children's accomplishments and continue to encourage them to pursue their dreams and career goals. We instilled in them from childhood that hard work and dedication will pay off, in the end. It is like planting a seed and seeing it grow and blossom.

Survival

Our marriage has definitely been through many highs and lows. We have shared so much over the years and we have grown. There were many times we did not know if we would make it. There were times when we wanted to quit. There have been times when I could not stand seeing him or being around him and I know he felt the same way.

I can remember times when I just wanted to be completely free from marriage. I felt like I was trapped and there was no escape. Sometimes I felt that I am the only person in the world has been married for so long and have been true and faithful to my husband. I actually felt like something must be wrong with me for staying married so long.

Even though my parents were basically married forever, I said to myself, who does that in these times. Forgetting that the world changes but God's word does not. It was at those times, when my husband and I will not get along, that I wanted him out of my life.

I did not care if I never saw his face again or heard his voice. I just wanted to be free. I wanted to go back in time and experience my youth and the things I felt I missed. The Devil is a liar. Moving forward is what we must do not look back.

In those times, I looked internally and I found my happy place. A place where I can go to and no one knew what I felt but God and me. I guess this is what it means to enter into your closet and shut the door, so you can have that one and one time with God, to tell him all that you feel even though he already knows.

Therefore, it was during those times, when Mr. T. would come home, I would deliberately pick an argument and be mean to him. He felt like I did not want him around and he would come home and not speak to me but stayed downstairs in the couch. I will close my bedroom door and shut him out. At times, I even put his clothes out of my closet in a spare bedroom.

Then, there were those times, when I anticipated him coming home and when I hear the door open, my heart would leap. When he called out my name or my special name that he calls me, I would smile then I would go down stairs. He would look at me and smile.

We have such a rich history, and even though it has not been a bed of roses, it is our history, it is our story and we love the memories and the life we have built for us and our kids. No one can take away those memories they will be forever in our hearts. We know it has not been easy but we have always had each other's back.

We are the lovebirds as we are sometimes called by close friends and we enjoy each other. Even when we are fighting, we fight with passion, we tease with passion and we makeup with passion.

We are a passionate couple. When we fight there is so much fun in making up, I think we fight just to make up. I am sure all of you experience the same. Sometimes you are driven to start something, knowing how it would eventually end.

We have been best friends and there were times we lost that and did not even feel like friends. We felt like strangers, but the power of prayer is strong. The power of the word is strong and when you know who you believe in, you can overcome the negative and turn it into good.

We have indeed done just that. For despite all the negativity and those who said we were not going to last a year, well here we are still together. There has been so much time of joy and laughter.

We look forward to vacation and there have been so many vacation trips; so many lovely and passionate moments that sustained us through those horrible times of feeling unloved and neglected. Those are the times that we treasure. Those are precious times that are irreplaceable and will last a lifetime.

There has been so much family fun time with our children, to the various amusement parks. Watching them grow, evolve and become their own individual person has been a blessing and we are grateful. There have been so many fun-filled moments at home, just sitting and watching television or making jokes on and of each other.

Yes, there have also been so many mommy and daddy jokes; lots of sibling jokes. So much precious times spent with each other. The good definitely surpasses the bad and through it all we have endured and are standing on solid ground.

We do not know what the future holds but we definitely know who holds the future.

There have been beautiful Christian moments in the church. There has been great fellowship with friends and family. We cannot see ourselves without each other. We do not want to be without each other.

After all this time, we are still in love. Yes, we still love each other deeply and passionately and want the best for each other. At times we are sad but for the most part we are very happy. For the most part, we encourage each other to hold on and not give up.

We are stronger and happier together than we are apart. Are there times of doubts? Yes, every now and then, the enemy will try to interfere, but greater is he who is within us than he that is in the world.

Are there times that I feel like I hate him and times I feel he hates me? Yes there are. However it is not really hate, it is frustration and sometimes disappointments but we know it is not hate.

Just like any couple, there are times when we feel we are being lied to. Can any one say they have never lied? Can any one say they have never twisted the truth? Of course not, and if you say yes, you are lying.

We are one and our marriage is not perfect but we work hard every day to perfect it or to bring it closer to perfection. We do have a lot of work to do, but we know that God has brought us this far and he will see us through more tough times, that may be ahead.

As previously stated, we do not know what the future holds, but we indeed know who holds the future. You do not get to decide what happens to us, God does, and we trust him implicitly. The only thing that is left for you to do is to pray for us that God will continue to bless us that we may bless others.

My Advice to Mr. & Mrs. Todman

Honey, I have provided advice to my friends and it is only fitting for me to also share some of that advice with us. So, in the event we have stopped, let us resume the following:

Pray for each other and with each other.

Spend quality time with each other.

Remain best friends. Do not shut each other out.

Keep the communication line open.

Trust each other even in difficult situations.

Be faithful and loyal to each other.

Do not let anyone interfere with our marriage.

Be happy. Love, laugh, play, sing, dance and let us continue to have each other's back.

The greatest gift from God is love, so let us enjoy it and remember how much and how long we have loved each other. Let us be a blessing to others and to each other. Love You!!!

Chapter XIII

Conclusion

Readers, we have traveled through a journey of the good, bad, and the estranged. We have learned from each couple through their struggles and their triumphs.

I am hoping that the Internal/External questions have helped you to examine some difficult and burning questions that may not be easy to acknowledge.

In addition, I am hoping that the questions on our cheating radar alert have awaken you to be aware of what your spouses do or not do and how they conduct themselves. These questions were asked to help you to examine and pay attention to your spouses behaviors so you are not left in the dark and clueless.

The Fence's Family, with all the women in the world, Mr. Fence chose to cheat on Mrs. Fence, with the caregivers they employed, doing the act right on their property. It was interesting to observe he was hiring the ones he wanted to be with. Despite the warning signs, Mrs. Fence decided to ignore them.

Please do not let that happen to you and you remain in denial. That is not a healthy state to be in. Keep your eyes open at all times and know what is going on around you.

Let us look at the Perfect Family. This family seemed to be as perfect as they are cute. No one would be the wiser that Mr. Perfect would cheat on a beautiful person like Mrs. Perfect. The question remains, why men cheat when they have everything they need at home.

Though it was painful to admit, Mrs. Perfect had to come to terms, after Mr. Perfect admitted his infidelity. Too bad, he had to be hospitalized to realize what he was doing was wrong.

As Christians, God will do whatever needs to be done to bring us back to that place where he needs us to be. We cannot play with God. If we are Christians we need to live the life that God has called us to live, which is to be a witness to others.

The good thing is, the Perfect's rekindled their love for each other, their faith in God and they are living a beautiful life, loving each other, serving God and raising their children together.

How about the Markers? As successful as you are, money does not buy love. Maybe it is possible that people grow out of love. If Mr. Markers has stopped loving Mrs. Markers as a husband should love his wife, he should come clean and tell her, so she can make an informed decision.

In the interim, I hope they find a way to communicate and work on their marriage so it can be at least close to what it used to be. Chances are it will not be the same, but miracles do happen so it can get better.

As for the Wonderful's, they experienced infidelity on both sides, but they rose above it. They however, are happier than they have ever been. "Love is in fact a beautiful thing".

They are doing financially well and enjoying God's blessings in their lives. In addition, they know that there may be challenging times ahead and they may be tempted, but they are also aware that they do not have to yield to temptation. May God continue to bless them as they stay in his "Word".

What Can I say about the Lyer's, or the former Lyer's? I am indeed happy for Mrs. Lyer and I am sure she will find her soul mate and be happy. She is still young as age is only a number.

As long as you have breath, you are never too old to find your soul mate. With what she has been through, she deserves a second chance. The good thing is, she does not need to depend on a man for financial support and that is a blessing.

Wherever, Mr. Lyer is, I am sure he is probably lying to an innocent young lady and trying to pull the wool over her eyes, like he did with his spouse. My hope for him is that he will recommit himself to Christ. In the event he finds someone, I pray that he will be faithful and treat her with utmost respect and devotion.

How can we forget the Fireworks? They do cause some fireworks. Mr. Fireworks having multiple affairs, on his end and Mrs. Fireworks, one, on her end, seemed like there would be no end to the infidelity. Therefore, I applaud Mrs.

Fireworks for confronting the wrongdoer, so the wrong can be made right.

I must commend Mr. Fireworks for his willingness to face the mistress with his wife by his side and let her know it is over. If you cannot face the person and let your spouse know who that person is, you are not ready to be free.

They have overcome many obstacles so I do believe their love will continue to grow as they remain faithful to each other. It is not going to be easy but they are the Fireworks, so all will be ok.

The Wright's of course, is the couple that everyone admires and desires to be like. They indeed have it together. We all can agree that they have a marriage made in heaven. Therefore, they actually have a little piece of heaven on earth. I know they will continue to be loyal to each other and we will continue to admire them.

Mr. & Ms. Fantasy, I am sure will remain to be just that, a fantasy. They may have desires and feelings for each other, but I do think they know the risks involved and the pain it will cause; for that, they will keep it what it is, a fantasy.

I do get the feeling the only way they will cross the line, is if both of them become single. After all this time, I think it is only then, they may re-entertain the idea of being together. They are older and wiser, but an affair is an affair, emotional or physical.

Last but not least, what do I say to Mr. T. and myself? We have been through it all and we are still standing. We wanted to quit many times, but we hang on to each other and to the promise that God will never leave or forsake us.

In addition, we know that we are in it for the "long-haul" and many may try to break us, but they have to go through God to get to us. We find comfort in knowing that "greater is he that is in us than he that is in the world".

I am so glad and fulfilled that I was able to compete this book on a positive note. I can truly say writing a book is like a journey that you go through. You may start on one road and end up on another.

In addition, I am thankful, that though I have been through the fire and rain in my marriage and thought many times that I would walk away, even during the course of writing this book, as I had no idea what would be my closing, it is a blessing to say that I am still with my Mr. T.

We look forward to many more joyful years together and know that God will continue to richly bless us. As married couples, you do the same. Look forward to many years of happiness and blessings with your spouses.

Marriage is like an investment. You invest time, and make many sacrifices. Through it all you endure the good, the bad, and the estranged. You get out of your marriage, what you put into it. Let us love our spouses the way we expect to be loved and give each other 100%, everything that we have, withholding nothing.

We know when it is bad it is really bad, but when it is good it is superlative. Yes, I know you agree, and if we commit our selves to Christ and to each other, treat each other with respect, communicate effectively, become and/or remain best friends, honor, love, and trust each other completely, we will never have to ask the question, "who cheats more than a politician?"

Thank you for reading.

V.T. Author

www.ingramcontent.com/pod-product-compliance
Lightning Source LLC
Chambersburg PA
CBHW021231090426
42740CB00006B/480